LOW CHOLESTEROL COOKBOOK FOR BEGINNERS

1500 Days of Easy & Delicious Recipes to Lower Your Cholesterol, Improve Heart Health and Live a Healthy Life.
Includes 30-Day Meal Plan

Laura Kelley

ISBN: **979-8355517083**

10 9 8 7 6 5 4 3 2 1

GET YOUR BONUS NOW!

Hello! First of all, I would like to thank you for purchasing the "LOW CHOLESTEROL COOKBOOK FOR BEGINNERS" I'm sure it will be very useful to improve your heart health and overall well-being!. To prove my gratitude for the trust you have placed in my experience, I am so happy to gift you with another one of my books, "MEDITERRANEAN DIET COOKBOOK,"
which I am sure will make your health explode. Don't wait any longer, follow the instructions below to download the digital version for free! Enjoy your reading!

MEDITERRANEAN DIET COOKBOOK
800 Quick, Easy, and Mouthwatering Recipes with Easy-to-Follow Instructions to Help You Weight Loss and Regain Vitality.
30-Day Meal Plan Included

The bonus is **100% free**, with no strings attached.
You don't need to enter any details except your name and email address.

To download your bonuses scan the QR code below or go to

https://books-bonuses.com/laura-kelley-bonuses-hh

Table of Contents

Introduction

Thousands of people yearly are diagnosed with high cholesterol, increasing the risk of circulatory problems, heart disease and strokes. The likelihood is if you are reading this book that, you or a family member is one of them. Or maybe you are at risk and want to prevent diseases linked with high cholesterol. Then this Quick Start Guide is for you! You can take charge of your health and lower your cholesterol.

Things have changed dramatically recently, and the previous advice is no longer valid. New research shows that many foods we were told to avoid do not hurt blood cholesterol. That will come as welcome news, especially if you avoided the foods you love and still have high cholesterol, despite your best efforts.

There are plenty of products on the market to reduce cholesterol, yet we unwittingly eat foods raising our bad cholesterol every day, so the problem isn't going away. Certain foods are best avoided completely. Once you know what that means, a healthy, balanced diet is the way forward. The excellent news is that delicious everyday foods naturally lower your cholesterol, so the diet is not so much about restriction but expanding your diet. By incorporating these beneficial foods into your diet, you can lower your cholesterol and, more, do it naturally.

In this book, we bring you the essential information based on the newest findings in a comprehensive, easy-to-understand way, providing you with what you need to know to help you reduce your cholesterol, with plenty of tips plus plenty of delicious everyday recipes which mostly consist of store cupboard ingredients which are easy to source. You'll discover how you can positively impact your future health by taking simple, straightforward steps. Whether you currently have high cholesterol, are borderline, or are concerned due to a family history of raised cholesterol or heart disease, it's never too soon to take action. Read on if you are ready to make positive changes to your or your family's health!

What Is Cholesterol?

Cholesterol is a fatty molecule that is present in your bloodstream. Although your body needs cholesterol to produce healthy cells, excessive cholesterol levels may raise your risk of heart disease.

High cholesterol might cause fatty deposits in your blood vessels. These deposits eventually accumulate, making it harder for adequate blood to circulate through your arteries. These deposits may rupture unexpectedly and create a clot, resulting in a heart attack or stroke.

High cholesterol may be inherited, but it is more typically the consequence of poor lifestyle choices, making it both avoidable and curable. High cholesterol may be reduced by a nutritious diet, frequent exercise, and, in some cases, medication.

Cholesterol is also obtained from animal products such as egg yolks, beef, and whole-milk dairy products. Too much cholesterol in the blood may cause plaque on blood vessel walls, obstruct blood flow to tissues and organs, and raise the risk of heart disease and stroke.

Types of Cholesterol

Chylomicrons: These lipoproteins are produced in the digestive system to carry triglycerides from our food. They are large in size.

Very Low-density Lipoproteins: These are another type of lipoproteins that carry triglycerides. While chylomicrons are produced in the intestines, VLDL is produced in the liver. Once the cells extract the triglycerides, the VLDLs turn to IDLs (intermediate-density lipoproteins) before changing to LDLs.

Intermediate Density Lipoproteins: These lipoproteins are produced when triglycerides are extracted from VLDL. They are removed from the body by the liver. Some VLDL is broken down and converted to LDL.

Low-density Lipoproteins: Since the triglycerides in VLDL are taken by the body cells, the LDL is mainly composed of cholesterol. It is referred to as bad cholesterol because it has to carry cholesterol from the liver to other parts of the body. Once it becomes too much in the blood, it leads to the accumulation of cholesterol.

High-Density Lipoproteins: These are called good cholesterol because they take cholesterol from other body parts down to the liver for excretion. The liver then converts the cholesterol to bile salt before releasing it into the bile, which is removed completely from the body.

If the liver fails to complete the cycle by removing the cholesterol sent by the HDL, it will accumulate cholesterol in the bloodstream, which could cause plaque buildup. As the plaque grows, it narrows the artery and affects the blood and oxygen supply rate to different body organs.

If blood flow to the heart is restricted, it increases the risk of heart disease such as heart attacks, angina, heart failure, etc. If the blood that goes to the brain is restricted, it can lead to stroke.

What Are the Symptoms of High Cholesterol?

Until there is an emergency, high cholesterol usually has no symptoms. A blood test is the only method to determine your high LDL cholesterol levels. Untreated cholesterol may lead to plaque formation over time, weakening the heart and putting you at risk for a heart attack or stroke. Keep an eye out for signs of a heart attack or an early stroke, such as:

- Nausea
- Numbness
- Flustered speech
- Extreme tiredness
- Angina or chest discomfort
- Breathing difficulties
- Extreme numbness or coldness
- Hypertension (high blood pressure)

If you have any worries about your symptoms, don't hesitate to go to the closest 24-hour emergency hospital. They may examine your blood work and do tests to confirm that nothing significant is wrong.

Discover what blood tests are performed in the emergency department.

How can you tell if you have high cholesterol without a blood test?

As previously said, you cannot tell you have high cholesterol unless you are in the middle of an emergency or have the results of a blood test. Lipid testing should begin between the ages of 9 and 11 and be repeated every five years until age 45 or 55, depending on gender.

Risk Factors of High Cholesterol

Heart disease risk factors fluctuate from person to person. Some persons may have high HDL/LDL ratios and blood cholesterol levels despite consuming a lot of saturated fats and cholesterol. Others have a hostile response to food and develop complications soon. To combat the condition with the right diet, exercise, and prescription drug balance, it's critical first to recognize your particular risk factors.

a. Family History

Family history is one of the most important indicators or predictors of developing heart disease. The amount of cholesterol your body generates each day is regulated by your genes. You can't change your genes, but you can improve your health by treating your body well. Your liver generates between 800 and 1000 milligrams of cholesterol daily, significantly more than you can consume. Because cholesterol is a necessary component of life, your body ensures that you always have enough. You don't need to consume any cholesterol; your body produces enough to keep you healthy. Familial hypercholesterolemia is a genetic abnormality that causes the body to create higher LDL cholesterol, despite diet and exercise. To help regulate cholesterol levels, people with this mutation must typically rely on prescription medicines.

b. Smoking

Smoking is not allowed. If you smoke, you should try to quit as soon as possible because it raises LDL cholesterol and lowers HDL cholesterol, and inflammation is also a consequence. Cigarette smoke includes about 4,000 chemicals, including at least 43 carcinogens classified as class C. It also boosts the clotting mechanism in the blood, leading to thrombosis, heart attack, or stroke.

c. Trans Fats Consumption

Trans fats are artificial food made by mixing hydrogen atoms with polyunsaturated fats. The body does not recognize the resulting molecule as a foreign object; it is incorporated into everything from cell membranes to hormones. This affects your health by altering the function of certain body parts. Trans fats enhance the amount of LDL cholesterol and should be strictly avoided. Consume many fresh foods, such as fruits, lean meats, dairy products, whole grains, and veggies. But, learn to read labels and avoid processed and quick meals. Even if the label says, "0 g trans-fat per serving," if the word hydrogenated appears in the ingredient list, the food contains trans-fat.

d. Sedentary Lifestyle

Even mild to moderate exercise in your weekly routine will help lower LDL cholesterol and raise HDL levels. The American Heart Association suggests thirty minutes of moderate exercise daily. However, you do not have to work out for thirty minutes in a row. For the same health benefit, break it up into three ten-minute sessions. Before starting an exercise regimen, ensure your doctor's approval. Begin slowly. After a tough exercise, nothing destroys your determination like very painful muscles. Your objective is to be able to work out the next day.

You will have health issues if your cholesterol level is too low. Low cholesterol levels may cause depression and anxiety because serotonin levels in the brain are reduced. People with extremely low cholesterol levels (below 100 mg/dL) are more likely to have suicidal thoughts and violence.

e. Obesity

Maintain or improve a healthy weight and BMI. Compare your height to the weight ranges on charts provided by insurance companies. Being overweight is defined as carrying more than 20% of your body weight over the highest weight for your height. Obesity is defined as a proportion of your body weight exceeding 30%.

f. Sodium

People consume much too much sodium in their diets. One issue is that salt is included in many processed meals and restaurant cuisine. This "invisible" salt is often sufficient to fulfill our daily needs. It's tough to cut salt out of your diet since it's naturally found in many foods and is utilized in large amounts in processed meals. Read labels carefully and track how much sodium you ingest in a day. The entire number will surprise you!

If you truly like the taste of salt, consider sprinkling a tiny quantity on your dish before you eat it. The salt will contact your taste receptors rapidly in this manner, making the meal taste saltier. Salt can be replaced by herbs, spices, and acidic components like lemon and vinegar. According to studies, people who eat a low-salt diet have a 20% reduced risk of heart disease and a 20% lower risk of dying from a heart attack. It will take some time and effort to switch to a low-salt diet. This may be tough at first since our taste receptors are used to salt; people begin to want salt as early as four months of life. However, after a time, you'll notice that less salt makes meals taste better, and many processed items will taste overly salty.

g. Poor Diet

A diet high in processed foods and low in fruits and vegetables leads to the development of heart disease. People prefer fast and highly processed foods to save time due to their hectic lives. Our health has suffered as we have moved away from whole foods.

How To Lose Weight on The Low Cholesterol Diet.

A low-cholesterol diet is a healthy way to lose weight. You'll need to eat fewer calories than you would on a traditional diet to follow the diet, and you'll also need to be watchful of your food choices. You can choose from various foods that fit this dietary pattern and find them at most health food stores or online.

To ensure you're getting enough calories, start by eating about 2,000 calories per day on the low-cholesterol diet. This number will increase as you lose weight, so keep track of how many calories you're consuming and adjust your intake accordingly.

In addition to eating plenty of nutritious foods, it's important to drink plenty of water and get enough exercise. The exercise portion of the low-cholesterol diet will require much more energy than a regular diet, but it will help you drop pounds quickly. Exercise helps burn off excess fat and promotes healthy skin and hair.

Foods To Eat

Different foods can decrease the level of cholesterol in different ways. Some offer soluble fiber that binds cholesterol and pushes it out of the body before it gets to your blood circulation. There are some which give you polyunsaturated fats, which directly decrease the level of your LDL. And some have plant stanols and sterols, which block the system from absorbing too much cholesterol.

a. Oatmeal

An easy way to start your new low cholesterol-friendly diet is to have a bowl of oatmeal or cold oatmeal-based cereal for your breakfast. Oats are known to provide you with 1 to 2 grams of soluble fiber. You may want slices of banana or berries to make it tastier. It is recommended to get 20 to 35 grams of fiber daily, with at least 5 to 10 grams of soluble fiber.

b. Barley And Other Whole Grains

Like oatmeal, barley, and other whole grain foods help lower the risk of heart complications, generally through the soluble fiber they give.

c. Beans

Beans particularly contain a high amount of soluble fiber. It also takes a while for the body to digest, which means you'll feel full for longer. That is one good reason beans are beneficial food for those who want to shed weight. With many choices and ways to prepare them, beans are a versatile food to add to your diet.

d. Nuts

Many studies reveal that eating walnuts, almonds, peanuts, and other nuts are good for the heart. Eating 2 ounces of nuts daily, you're helping your body slightly lower its LDL level, 5% or more. Nuts have extra nutrients that guard the heart in many other ways.

e. Okra And Eggplant

These two low-calorie vegetables should be added to your diet as they are great sources of soluble fiber.

f. Vegetable Oils

Using liquid vegetable oils like sunflower, canola, safflower, and others instead of lard, butter, or shortening is helpful to lower LDL.

g. Foods Rich With Stanols And Sterols

Stanols and sterols extracted from plants sap up the ability of the body to absorb food cholesterol. Many companies add them to foods ranging from granola bars and margarine to chocolate and orange juice. They are also available in supplements. Consuming 2 grams of plant stanols and sterols daily will lower LDL cholesterol by approximately 10%.

h. Apples, Strawberries, Grapes, And Citrus Fruits

These fruits have a high level of pectin, a type of soluble fiber that helps lower LDL.

i. Soy

Eating soybeans and foods made of them, such as soy milk and tofu, were once flaunted as a great way to lower the body's cholesterol level. Studies show that it has a more modest effect on the body— when you consume 25 grams of soy protein daily, it can lower LDL by 5% to 6%.

j. Fiber Supplements

Natural supplements offer the least pleasing way to acquire soluble fiber. About two teaspoons a day of psyllium found in Metamucil and other bulk-developing laxatives offer approximately 4 grams of good soluble fiber.

k. Fatty Fish

Eating fish at least 2 or 3 times a week can lower LDL in two ways: by substituting meat, which contains LDL-improving saturated fats, and by offering LDL-lowering omega-3 fats. Omega-3s lessen triglycerides in the arteries and guard the heart by helping stop the onset of irregular heartbeats.

Foods To Avoid

Some dietitians advise shoppers to avoid specific grocery aisles. For example, bypass aisles contain bakery products, crackers, cookies, and other high-saturated-fat meals. In general, avoid the following products if they show prominently on the ingredient list of a food label:

a. Trans fats

These are unhealthy and can be found in packaged treats such as pastries, cookies, crackers, and certain margarine. Read the nutrition data to find out about all the fats in the product. For example, biscuits, breakfast sandwiches, microwave popcorn, cream-filled confectionery, doughnuts, fried fast meals, and frozen pizza are high in trans fats.

b. Red Meats

Steak, beef roast, ribs, pork chops, and ground beef are rich in saturated fat and cholesterol.

Choose 90% lean ground beef, lean beef cuts (such as sirloin, tenderloin, filet or flank steak, pork loin, or tenderloin), and lower-fat animal protein sources such as baked skinless or lean ground chicken.

c. Poultry Skin

While poultry skin may not have as much saturated fat as red meat, it still has a substantial quantity. Compared to only the flesh, a chicken thigh with the skin contains almost 2 g more saturated fat. And in this instance, getting rid of the fat is simple—just don't eat the skin.

d. Salt

Too much salt might contribute to high blood pressure. You're undoubtedly aware that canned soup and salty snack items are bad for you. However, did you know that it may also be found in bread and rolls, cold cuts and cured meats, pizza, poultry, and fast-food sandwiches?

You might also be shocked at how common it is in frozen meals. When in doubt, always read the labels. Avoid taking moreover 2,300 to 2,400 mg per day.

e. Sugar

Yes, it's delicious. However, too much may cause weight gain, heart disease, diabetes, and cholesterol issues. Of course, it's easier said than done, so try to minimize how much of this you consume.

Many of the "usual suspects" are certainly familiar to you: soda, sweet tea, candies, cakes, cookies, and ice cream, to name a few. But did you know that sugar is added to foods you would not think of, such as spaghetti sauce and fast food? Many tomatoes, ketchup, breakfast bars, and tonic waterfall into this category. Because the components are listed by weight, from most to least, it's best to concentrate on the first three to five. Be wary of prepared foods that promote a single component; instead, look at the entire packaging. Speak with your doctor or a nutritionist about further strategies to enhance your diet.

f. Egg Yolks

Single egg yolk has 214 mg of cholesterol, more than two-thirds of the daily limit. Use can't make an egg replacement or egg whites instead of whole eggs.

Eggs' cholesterol gets a bad rap. One egg contains approximately 60% of the daily value for cholesterol but only 8% of saturated fat. Eggs are strong in protein, low in calories, and rich in B vitamins, iron, and anti-inflammatory minerals. If you must limit your cholesterol intake, stick to egg whites, which are high in protein but low in cholesterol.

Performing Regular Exercise to Lowers Cholesterol

Though many people know how important exercise is in improving the body's health, many are unaware of how it contributes to increasing the levels of LDL and, at the same time, decreasing the levels of HDL. Simply performing an aerobic exercise can help the body raise its HDL level, which is necessary to protect you against severe health conditions like heart disease.

Exercise is very important. Exercise comes with cardiovascular benefits along with weight loss benefits. Committing to 60 minutes of moderate exercise on a regular day is recommended to lose weight.

Activities such as bicycling, brisk walking, dancing, swimming, gardening, aerobics, and jogging will provide cardio benefits.

a. How Exercise Lowers Cholesterol

Nutritionists believe there are some tools involved. First, exercise boosts the enzymes that help move LDL from the bloodstream to the liver. The cholesterol is turned into bile or defecated. So, the more physical activities you do, the lower your LDL.

Secondly, exercise boosts the size of the protein elements that transmit cholesterol through the bloodstream. Some elements are dense and small; some are fleecy and big. The dense, small elements are more precarious than the fluffy, big ones, as the smaller ones can squeeze into the blood vessels and heart coatings. But now, it shows that exercise can boost the size of the protein elements that convey both bad and good lipoproteins.

b. How Much Physical Exercise Do You Exactly Need?

Even though the National Health Association has suggested that 150 minutes of exercise a week is necessary for good cholesterol, the exact amount of exercise necessary to lower the cholesterol level is still under debate.

A study performed in 2002 by researchers at Duke University Medical Center in the US revealed that hardcore exercise is essentially better than moderate exercise to lower cholesterol. In research done on overweight people who are inactive and have a bad diet, they found that people who got moderate exercise lowered their LDL levels. But those who did heavier exercise lowered it a lot more.

People who exercised strongly also elevated their HDL levels. Researchers found that it requires much high-power exercise to change the HDL level suggestively, and a restful walk wouldn't make a big difference.

But findings suggested that although the moderate exercise wasn't as effective in decreasing the levels of LDL or increasing the levels of HDL, it is still good in preventing the boost of cholesterol levels.

So, a small exercise is better than no exercise at all; but the more exercise, the better.

To improve cholesterol levels, on top of decreasing your blood pressure and possibly having strokes and heart attack, the American Heart Association suggests an average of 40 minutes of moderate to vigorous physical activity 3 or 4 times a week. For total cardiovascular wellbeing, the American Heart Association recommends at least 2½ hours of moderate exercise or 1¼ hours of strong exercise per week. You can combine vigorous and moderate activity if you would like.

Examples of moderate exercise include:

- Walking rapidly
- Riding bicycling
- Playing sports like tennis or basketball
- Performing house chores like gardening

Examples of vigorous exercise include:

- Jogging or running on a treadmill
- Hiking and trekking uphill
- Swimming
- Aerobic dancing
- Playing sports like tennis
- Bicycling

Taking a test is the easiest way to define if you are working out at a positive level. According to the American Heart Association, for moderate exercise, you must be able to engage in a conversation; throughout vigorous activities, you must stop to take a breath after talking.

You can also use special gadgets or simply your fingers to measure your pulse and find out if you are at your goal heart rate. To estimate your maximum heart rate, deduct your age from 220. The target heart rate is 50% to 85%.

Measuring Conversions

Weight (mass)	
Metric (grams)	US contemporary (ounces)
14 grams	½ ounce
28 grams	1 ounce
85 grams	3 ounces
100 grams	3.53 ounces
113 grams	4 ounces
227 grams	8 ounces
340 grams	12 ounces
454 grams	16 ounces or 1 pound

Volume (liquid)	
Metric	US Customary
.6 ml	⅛ tsp
1.2 ml	¼ tsp
2.5 ml	½ tsp
3.7 ml	¾ tsp
5 ml	1 tsp
15 ml	1 tbsp
30 ml	2 tbsp
59 ml	2 fluid ounces or ¼ cup
118 ml	½ cup
177 ml	¾ cup
237 ml	1 cup or 8 fluid ounces
1.9 liters	8 cups or ½ gallon

Oven Temperatures	
Metric	US contemporary
121° C	250° F
149° C	300° F
177° C	350° F
204° C	400° F
232° C	450° F

The table below shows normal lipogram ranges.

	Normal	High	Very high
Total cholesterol	< 5.2 mmol/l	5.2-6.2 mmol/l	> 6.2 mmol/l
LDL- cholesterol	< 3.3 mmol/l	3.3 – 4.1 mmol/l	> 4.1 mmol/l
HDL- cholesterol	> 1 mmol/l	1.1 – 1.6 mmol/l*	> 1.6 mmol/l*
Triglycerides	< 1.7 mmol/l	1.7 – 2.3 mmol/l	> 2.3 mmol/l

High HDL cholesterols are desirable. It is the formed cholesterol that removes it from the blood

CHAPTER 1: Breakfast

1. Protein Cereal

Difficulty: ★★☆☆☆
Preparation time: 5 minutes
Cooking time: 20 minutes
Servings: 4
Ingredients:

- 1¾ cups water
- 1 cup quinoa
- Pinch fine sea salt
- 1 cup raisins
- ½ cup almonds, roughly chopped
- 1 cup unsweetened almond milk
- 4 tsp organic honey

Directions:

1. Add the water, quinoa, and salt to boil in a medium stockpot.
2. Bring the heat down to low, then simmer, covered, for 15 minutes, or until the water is absorbed. Remove from the heat and let it rest for 5 minutes.
3. Add the raisins and almonds, and mix to combine.
4. Place a ¾ cup of the quinoa mixture into four bowls and pour a ¼ cup of almond milk into each bowl. Drizzle each bowl of quinoa with 1 tsp of organic honey.

Per serving: Calories: 313kcal; Fat: 10g; Carbs: 48g; Protein: 10g; Saturated Fat: 1g; Cholesterol: 0mg; Sugar: 6g

2. Breakfast Splits

Difficulty: ★☆☆☆☆
Preparation time: 10 minutes
Cooking time: 0 minutes
Servings: 2
Ingredients:

- 2 tablespoons of low-fat yogurt
- 2 peeled bananas
- 4 tablespoons of granola
- 2 chopped strawberries
- ½ teaspoon of ground cinnamon

Directions:

1. Combine yogurt, ground cinnamon, and strawberries in a mixing dish. Then cut the bananas lengthwise and fill them with the yogurt mass. Granola may be sprinkled on top of the fruits.

Per serving: Calories: 154kcal; Fat: 8g; Carbs: 45g; Protein: 7g; Saturated Fat: 2g; Cholesterol: 1mg; Sugar: 3g

3. Cranberry Hotcakes

Difficulty: ★★☆☆☆
Preparation time: 5 minutes
Cooking time: 9 minutes
Servings: 2
Ingredients:

- 1 cup rolled oats
- 1 cup cranberries
- 3 tbsp. fat-free plain yoghurt
- ¼ cup unsweetened almond milk
- 1 tbsp. ground flaxseed
- 1 large egg
- ½ tsp ground cinnamon
- 2 tsp avocado oil

Directions:

1. Mix the oats, cranberries, yoghurt, almond milk, flax seeds, egg, and cinnamon in a mixing bowl until it becomes a thick batter.
2. Heat the avocado oil over medium-low heat in a large nonstick frying pan. Pour ¼ cup of the batter into the pan and fry for 2 to 3 minutes, or until bubbles start to form on top. Flip and fry for 2 minutes until lightly browned and fully cooked. Continue with the remaining batter.
3. Serve with your favorite toppings.

Per serving: Calories: 328kcal; Fat: 12g; Carbs: 41g; Protein: 13g; Saturated Fat: 3g; Cholesterol: 83mg; Sugar: 8g

4. Nutty Oat Cereal

Difficulty: ★★★☆☆
Preparation time: 5 minutes
Cooking time: 30 minutes
Servings: 4
Ingredients:

- Parchment paper
- 1 cup rolled oats
- 1 cup dried pumpkin seeds
- ½ cup unsalted mixed nuts, roughly chopped
- Pinch fine sea salt
- 1 tbsp. olive oil
- 2 cups unsweetened cashew milk
- 1 cup strawberries, chopped
- 1 cup blueberries

Directions:

1. Heat the oven to 300°F gas mark 2. Line a baking sheet with parchment paper.
2. In a medium-sized mixing bowl, add the oats, pumpkin seeds, nuts, salt, and olive oil, and combine.
3. Transfer the oat mixture onto the prepared baking sheet in a thin layer.
4. Bake for 30 minutes, mixing the oats halfway through cooking, until lightly browned. Remove and set aside to cool.
5. Serve with cashew milk, chopped strawberries, and blueberries.

Per serving: Calories: 460kcal; Fat: 32g; Carbs: 34g; Protein: 14g; Saturated Fat: 3g; Cholesterol: 14mg; Sugar: 1g

5. Vegetable Omelet

Difficulty: ★★☆☆☆
Preparation time: 5 minutes
Cooking time: 5 minutes
Servings: 2
Ingredients:

- 1/4 cup of onion; diced
- 1 tablespoon of olive oil
- 1/4 cup of green bell peppers; diced
- 2 ounces mushrooms; sliced
- 1/4 cup of zucchini; sliced
- 2 tablespoons of fat-free sour cream
- 1/2 cup of tomato; diced
- 2 ounces Swiss cheese; shredded
- 1 cup of egg substitute
- 2 tablespoons of water

Directions:

1. In a large pan, heat the olive oil and cook the mushrooms, zucchini, green bell pepper, onion, and tomato until tender, finishing with the tomato.
2. Combine the sour cream egg substitute, and whisk until frothy. Place an omelet pan or skillet over medium-high heat and coat with the nonstick veggie spray.
3. Fill the pan with the egg mixture. As it cooks, lift the sides to let the raw egg flow below. Cover half the eggs with cheese and sautéed veggies when almost set, then fold another half over. Cook the eggs until they are set.

Per serving: Calories: 263kcal; Fat: 13g; Carbs: 8g; Protein: 25g; Saturated Fat: 3g; Cholesterol: 17mg; Sugar: 5g

6. Avo Bruschetta

Difficulty: ★☆☆☆☆
Preparation time: 5 minutes
Cooking time: 5 minutes
Servings: 2
Ingredients:

- 1 tbsp. olive oil
- 2 large free-range eggs
- 1 ripe avocado, pitted, peeled, and mashed

- Two whole-wheat bread small slices, toasted
- Fine sea salt
- Ground black pepper
- Pinch red pepper flakes (optional)
- One large Roma tomato, thinly sliced

Directions:

1. Heat the olive oil in a nonstick frying pan over medium heat.
2. Gently crack the eggs into the pan and fry for 3 to 4 minutes, flip, and cook for an extra 30 seconds, or until it has reached your desired doneness. Remove from the heat.
3. Portion the avocado evenly between the toasted slices, and season with salt, pepper, and a pinch of red pepper flakes (if using).
4. Place the sliced tomatoes over the avocado, top with the fried egg, and enjoy.

Per serving: Calories: 411kcal; Fat: 28g; Carbs: 29g; Protein: 14g; Saturated Fat: 6g; Cholesterol: 13mg; Sugar: 6g

7. Maghrebi Poached Eggs

Difficulty: ★★★☆☆
Preparation time: 5 minutes
Cooking time: 25 minutes
Servings: 4
Ingredients:

- 1 tbsp. avocado oil
- 1 medium red bell pepper, chopped
- 1 (28 oz) can of low-sodium diced tomatoes
- 1 tsp ground cumin
- Fine sea salt
- Ground black pepper
- 4 large free-range eggs
- ¼ cup cilantro, chopped

Directions:

1. Heat the avocado oil in a large heavy-bottom pan over medium-high heat.
2. Add the red bell pepper and cook for 4 to 6 minutes, until softened.
3. Add the tomatoes with the juice and cumin. Cook for 10 minutes until the flavor comes together and the sauce has thickened. Season with salt and pepper to taste.
4. Use a huge spoon to make four depressions in the tomato mixture. Carefully crack an egg into each depression. Cover the pan and cook for 5 to 7 minutes, or until the eggs are cooked to your liking. Remove from the heat.
5. Divide into four bowls and garnish with chopped cilantro. Serve while hot.

Per serving: Calories: 146kcal; Fat: 9g; Carbs: 10g; Protein: 8g; Saturated Fat: 2g; Cholesterol: 0mg; Sugar: 7g

8. Tofu And Cucumber Spring Rolls

Difficulty: ★★★☆☆
Preparation time: 10 minutes
Cooking time: 20 minutes
Servings: 5 Rolls
Ingredients:

- ⅓ cup Tangy Soy Sauce
- Three tablespoons of nut butter (almond, cashew, or all-natural peanut butter)
- 6 ounces firm tofu, cut into 10 (½-inch wide) strips
- Five rehydrated rice paper wraps
- One cucumber, peeled and cut into sticks

Directions:

1. Preheat the oven to 425°F. Line a baking sheet with parchment paper & set it aside.

2. Mix the Tangy Soy Sauce and the nut butter in a small bowl until well blended.

3. Drizzle 2 to 3 tablespoons of the sauce mixture over the tofu strips. You'll have some sauce left over. You can use this for dipping.

4. Bring the tofu strips to the prepared baking sheet and bake for 20 minutes.

5. Place the rehydrated rice paper wraps on a flat surface.

6. Once the tofu is done cooking, place two strips of tofu and a few cucumber sticks in the center of one wrap.

7. Fold the sides of the rice paper over the filling, then tightly roll from the bottom until the wrap is sealed. Repeat with the other wraps.

8. Enjoy the spring rolls with the dipping sauce.

Per serving: Calories: 181kcal; Fat: 8g; Carbs: 20g; Protein: 9g; Saturated Fat: 1g; Cholesterol: 45mg; Sugar: 8g

9. Creamed Rice

Difficulty: ★★☆☆☆
Preparation time: 5 minutes
Cooking time: 20 minutes
Servings: 2
Ingredients:

- ½ cup brown basmati rice
- 2 cups water
- 1 cup unsweetened almond milk & extra for serving
- 1 tsp vanilla extract
- ⅛ tsp ground cinnamon
- Pinch fine sea salt
- ¼ cup dried raisins
- ¼ cup unsalted mixed nuts, chopped
- 2 tbsp. organic honey

Directions:

1. Place the basmati rice in a large-sized mixing bowl and add the water. Soak overnight in the refrigerator, then drain.

2. Add the soaked rice, water, almond milk, vanilla extract, cinnamon, and fine sea salt to a medium-sized stockpot and place over medium heat.

3. Boil the rice mixture, then reduce the heat to low. Simmer for 20 minutes 'til the rice is tender and most of the liquid has been absorbed, stirring frequently.

4. Remove the stockpot from the heat and mix in the raisins, nuts, and honey. Add extra almond milk if you prefer a thinner pudding.

5. Serve.

Per serving: Calories: 341kcal; Fat: 8g; Carbs: 64g; Protein: 6g; Saturated Fat: 1g; Cholesterol: 0mg; Sugar: 5g

10. Nuts And Seeds Trail Mix

Difficulty: ★☆☆☆☆
Preparation time: 5 minutes
Cooking time: 0 minutes
Servings: 5 cups
Ingredients:

- 1 cup salted pumpkin seeds or petites
- 1 cup unbranched almonds
- 1 cup unsalted sunflower kernels
- 1 cup walnut halves
- 1 cup dried apricots
- 1 cup dark chocolate chips

Directions:

1. Place all ingredients in a huge bowl; toss to combine. Store in an airtight container.

Per serving: Calories: 336kcal; Fat: 25g; Carbs: 22g; Protein: 11g; Saturated Fat: 5g; Cholesterol: 0mg; Sugar: 4g

11. Vegetarian Scramble

Difficulty: ★★☆☆☆
Preparation time: 5 minutes
Cooking time: 15 minutes
Servings: 1
Ingredients:

- 2 tsp olive oil
- ¼ cup red onion, chopped
- 1 cup cherry tomatoes, halved
- 1 cup baby spinach
- 10 oz firm tofu, crumbled
- ¼ cup low-fat cottage cheese
- 1 tsp oregano, chopped
- Himalayan pink salt
- Ground black pepper

Directions:

1. Heat the olive oil in a frypan over medium heat.
2. Add the chopped onion to the pan and fry for 3 minutes until translucent.
3. Add the tomato halves and baby spinach, and fry for 3 minutes until the spinach is wilted.
4. Add the tofu to the pan and gently mix using a rubber spatula for 7 minutes until warm.
5. Gently mix in the cottage cheese and oregano.
6. Season with salt and pepper, and serve warm.

Per serving: Calories: 201kcal; Fat: 1g; Carbs: 9g; Protein: 20g; Saturated Fat: 0g; Cholesterol: 2mg; Sugar: 7g

12. Rolled Oats Cereal

Difficulty: ★★☆☆☆

Preparation time: 5 minutes

Cooking time: 5 minutes

Servings: 4

Ingredients:

- 2 tbsp. plant-based butter, plus one tablespoon of unsalted butter
- 1 tbsp. organic honey
- ¾ cup rolled oats
- ⅓ cup walnuts, roughly chopped
- 1 tbsp. chia seeds
- 1 tbsp. hemp seeds

- 1 tbsp. ground flaxseed
- ½ tsp ground cinnamon
- Pinch fine sea salt
- 2 tbsp. dried cranberries
- 2 tbsp. raisins

Directions:

1. In a huge heavy bottom pan, melt the butter and honey over medium heat, and cook until bubbly.
2. Mix in the oats, walnuts, chia seeds, hemp seeds, flaxseed, cinnamon, and salt. Cook for 3-4 minutes, stirring 'til the oats and nuts start to brown. If the mixture is browning too fast, turn the heat down to low. Remove from the heat, add the cranberries and raisins, and mix to combine.
3. Eat the oat cereal immediately, cool it completely, and then store it in an airtight container.

Per serving: Calories: 230kcal; Fat: 3g; Carbs: 18g; Protein: 5g; Saturated Fat: 0g; Cholesterol: 8mg; Sugar: 5g

13. Lean Beef Lettuce Wraps

Difficulty: ★★☆☆☆

Preparation time: 5 minutes

Cooking time: 15 minutes

Servings: 4

Ingredients:

- 1 pound lean ground beef
- ½ white onion, diced
- ⅓ cup honey-garlic sauce
- 1 tablespoon white vinegar
- Ten large lettuce leaves were washed and dried

Directions:

1. Over high heat, cook the ground beef in a huge skillet for 10 minutes until browned. Drain the fat.
2. Add the onion, Honey-Garlic Sauce, and vinegar to the pan, and cook for 3 to 5

minutes. Evenly divide the beef mixture between the lettuce leaves and fold them over. Enjoy immediately.

Per serving: Calories: 172kcal; Fat: 2g; Carbs: 8g; Protein: 21g; Saturated Fat: 0g; Cholesterol: 31mg; Sugar: 6g

14. Egg Foo Young

Difficulty: ★★☆☆
Preparation time: 5 minutes
Cooking time: 10 minutes
Servings: 3
Ingredients:

- Cooking spray
- ½ medium red bell pepper, chopped
- ½ medium green bell pepper, chopped
- ¼ cup red onion, finely chopped
- ¼ cup Roma tomatoes, chopped
- ¼ cup lean ham, chopped
- 2½ cups large egg whites
- ½ tsp basil, chopped
- Fine sea salt
- Ground black pepper

Directions:

1. Spray a medium nonstick frying pan with cooking spray and place it over medium heat.
2. Add the red and green bell peppers, onion, tomato, and ham to the pan and fry for 4 minutes until tender.
3. Add the egg whites into the pan, over the ham mixture, and cook for 1 minute, until just beginning to set. Use a rubber spatula or turner and gently lift the edges of the setting egg whites, tilting the pan to allow any uncooked egg to run beneath. Continue this process for 3 minutes until all the egg whites are set.
4. Remove the pan from the heat and fold one side of the egg white omelet over the other.
5. Cut the omelet in half, sprinkled with chopped basil, and seasoned with fine

sea salt and ground black pepper. Serve warm.

Per serving: Calories: 215kcal; Fat: 2g; Carbs: 8g; Protein: 41g; Saturated Fat: 0g; Cholesterol: 15mg; Sugar: 5g

15. Italian Baked Omelet

Difficulty: ★★★☆
Preparation time: 5 minutes
Cooking time: 20 minutes
Servings: 2
Ingredients:

- Cooking spray
- Six large free-range egg whites
- ¼ cup unsweetened soy milk
- ½ tsp basil, chopped
- Himalayan pink salt
- Ground black pepper
- ¼ cup green beans, chopped
- ¼ cup red bell pepper, chopped
- ½ spring onion, chopped
- 2 tbsp. fat-free cheddar cheese, shredded

Directions:

1. Preheat the oven to 350 deg. F gas mark 4. Grease 2 medium ramekins with cooking spray and set aside.
2. Add the egg whites, soy milk, and basil to a medium-sized mixing bowl, and whisk until well blended. Season with salt and pepper and set aside.
3. Divide the green beans, red bell pepper, and spring onion between the two ramekins and pour in the egg white mixture. Top each ramekin with 1 tbsp. of cheddar cheese.
4. Bake for 15-20 minutes, 'til the baked omelet has puffed up and lightly browned. Serve hot.

Per serving: Calories: 126kcal; Fat: 2g; Carbs: 5g; Protein: 16g; Saturated Fat: 2g; Cholesterol: 10mg; Sugar: 4g

16. Nutritious Roasted Chickpeas

Difficulty: ★★★☆☆
Preparation time: 10 minutes
Cooking time: 14 minutes
Servings: 2
Ingredients:

- 14 oz can chickpeas, drained & rinsed
- 1 tsp dried oregano
- 1 tsp dried thyme
- 1 tsp dried rosemary
- 2 tbsp sesame oil
- 1 ½ tsp onion powder
- Pepper
- Salt

Directions:

1. In a mixing bowl, toss chickpeas with oil, onion powder, rosemary, thyme, oregano, pepper, and salt until well coated.
2. Transfer chickpeas into the air fryer basket and cook at 370 F for 14 minutes. Stir halfway through.
3. Serve and enjoy.

Per serving: Calories: 369kcal; Fat: 16g; Carbs: 48g; Protein: 10g; Saturated Fat: 4g; Cholesterol: 0mg; Sugar: 8g

CHAPTER 2: Fish And Seafoods

17. Honey Soy Tilapia

Difficulty: ★★★☆☆
Preparation time: 10 minutes
Cooking time: 45 minutes
Servings: 2
Ingredients:

- 3 tbsps. honey
- 3 tbsps. soy sauce
- 3 tbsps. balsamic vinegar
- 1 tbsp. minced garlic
- 2 (3 oz.) fillets of tilapia
- cooking spray
- 1 tsp. freshly cracked black pepper

Directions:

1. Combine garlic, balsamic vinegar, soy sauce, and honey in a bowl. Add tilapia fillets to the mixture, and put in the fridge to marinate for a minimum of 30 minutes.
2. Turn the oven to 350°F (175°C) to preheat. Spray cooking spray over a baking dish.
3. Take the tilapia out of the marinade and dispose of the marinade. On the prepared cookie sheet, put the fillets and sprinkle over the fish with black pepper.
4. Bake in the oven for 15-20 minutes until a fork can easily flake the fish.

Per serving: Calories: 218kcal; Fat: 2g; Carbs: 33g; Protein: 19g; Saturated Fat: 0g; Cholesterol: 31mg; Sugar: 3g

18. Salmon Salad

Difficulty: ★★☆☆☆
Preparation time: 10 minutes
Cooking time: 0 minutes
Servings: 4
Ingredients:

- 1 diced white onion,
- 1-pound broiled salmon fillet,
- 1 cup of chopped spinach,
- 1 cup of chopped lettuce,
- One tablespoon of lemon juice
- 1 teaspoon of ground paprika
- 1 teaspoon of olive oil

Directions:

1. Combine the onion, spinach, lettuce, salmon fillet, and paprika in a salad bowl. Shake the ingredients vigorously. The salad should then be drizzled with lemon juice and olive oil.

Per serving: Calories: 177kcal; Fat: 8g; Carbs: 4g; Protein: 23g; Saturated Fat: 4g; Cholesterol: 20mg; Sugar: g

19. Citrus Swordfish With Citrus Salsa

Difficulty: ★★★☆☆
Preparation time: 10 minutes
Cooking time: 45 minutes
Servings: 6
Ingredients:

- One orange, peeled, sectioned, and cut into bite-size
- 1/2 cup canned pineapple chunks, undrained
- 1/4 cup diced fresh mango
- 2 jalapeno peppers, seeded and minced
- 3 tbsps. orange juice
- 1 tbsp. diced red bell pepper
- 2 tsps. white sugar
- 1 tbsp. chopped fresh cilantro
- 1/2 cup fresh orange juice
- 1 tbsp. olive oil
- 1/4 tsp. cayenne pepper
- 1 tbsp. pineapple juice concentrate, thawed

- 1 1/2 lbs. swordfish steaks

Directions:

1. To prepare the salsa: mix cilantro, sugar, diced red bell pepper, and 3 tbsps. of orange juice, minced jalapenos, mango, pineapple chunks, and oranges in a medium-sized bowl. Refrigerate, covered.

2. Combine pineapple juice concentrate, cayenne pepper, olive oil, and 1/2 cup of orange juice in a non-reactive bowl. Put swordfish steaks in the bowl, and flip to cover well. Let the swordfish marinate in the mixture for 30 minutes.

3. Prepare an outside grill, grease the rack set and put it 6 inches away from the heat source. If using a gas grill, set the gas grill to medium-high heat.

4. Grill each side of the swordfish until translucent in the middle, about 12-15 minutes. Enjoy the grilled fish with salsa.

Per serving: Calories: 214kcal; Fat: 7g; Carbs: 14g; Protein: 23g; Saturated Fat: 2g; Cholesterol: 44mg; Sugar: 3g

20. Fish Tacos

Difficulty: ★★★☆☆
Preparation time: 5 minutes
Cooking time: 20 minutes
Servings: 4
Ingredients:

- 1 lb white fish (such as tilapia), cut into bite-size pieces
- 1 tablespoon olive oil
- Sea salt
- Freshly ground black pepper
- 1 cup low-fat plain Greek yogurt
- 5 (6½-inch) whole wheat or whole-grain corn tortillas
- 2½ cups shredded romaine lettuce

- 2 tablespoons freshly squeezed lime juice

Directions:

1. Preheat the oven to 375°F. Line a baking sheet with parchment paper.

2. Season the fish with olive oil, salt, & pepper. Place the fish on the prepared baking sheet and bake for 20 minutes until slightly golden brown.

3. While the fish is cooking, combine the yogurt with another pinch of salt and pepper in a small bowl.

4. Once the fish is cooked, place ⅕ of the fish in a tortilla with ½ cup romaine, one teaspoon lime juice, and a dollop of yogurt. Repeat with the remaining tortillas, then serve immediately.

Per serving: Calories: 272kcal; Fat: 7g; Carbs: 29g; Protein: 23g; Saturated Fat: 2g; Cholesterol: 34mg; Sugar: 3g

21. Maple-Garlic Salmon And Cauliflower Sheet Pan Dinner

Difficulty: ★★★☆☆
Preparation time: 5 minutes + 30 minutes to marinate
Cooking time: 20 minutes
Servings: 4
Ingredients:

- 1 pound salmon fillet
- Three tablespoons minced garlic, divided
- 2 tablespoons olive oil, divided
- 2 tablespoons low-sodium soy sauce
- Freshly ground black pepper
- 2½ cups bite-size cauliflower florets
- Pinch sea salt
- 1½ tablespoons maple syrup

Directions:

1. Place the salmon, two tablespoons garlic, one tablespoon oil, soy sauce, and pepper in a resealable plastic bag and

place the bag in the refrigerator. Let the fish marinate for 30 mins or overnight.

2. Preheat the oven to 425°F. Line a baking sheet with parchment paper.

3. In a medium bowl, toss the cauliflower with the remaining olive oil, garlic, more pepper, and a pinch of salt, and place it on half the prepared baking sheet.

4. Place the marinated salmon on the other half of the sheet and bake for 20 minutes until the fish is slightly golden brown on the edges and just cooked through. Transfer the fish from the baking sheet to a plate and loosely cover it with foil to keep it warm. Flip the cauliflower and bake for 10 minutes more, until soft.

5. Drizzle the maple syrup over the salmon and serve with the cauliflower.

Per serving: Calories: 216kcal; Fat: 11g; Carbs: 9g; Protein: 20g; Saturated Fat: 2g; Cholesterol: 21mg; Sugar: 6g

22. Spicy Trout Sheet Pan Dinner

Difficulty: ★★☆☆☆
Preparation time: 5 minutes
Cooking time: 20 minutes
Servings: 4
Ingredients:

- Three tablespoons minced garlic, divided
- Two tablespoons chili powder, divided
- 2 tablespoons olive oil, divided
- Sea salt
- 1 pound rainbow trout fillets
- Two zucchini, sliced into rounds

Directions:

1. Preheat the oven to 425°F. Line a baking sheet with parchment paper.

2. Mix 2 tablespoons of garlic, one tablespoon of chili powder, one tablespoon of olive oil, and a pinch of salt. Generously coat both sides of the trout fillets with the garlic mixture and

place them on one half of the baking sheet.

3. Mix the remaining garlic, chili powder, olive oil, and another pinch of salt in another medium bowl. Add the zucchini to the bowl, then stir to combine.

4. Bake the fish for 20 minutes until slightly browned on the edges. Add the zucchini to the empty side of the baking sheet halfway through the cooking time. Enjoy immediately.

Per serving: Calories: 186kcal; Fat: 9g; Carbs: 6g; Protein: 20g; Saturated Fat: 2g; Cholesterol: 17mg; Sugar: 2g

23. Grilled Scallops With Gremolata

Difficulty: ★★★☆☆
Preparation time: 15 minutes
Cooking time: 6 minutes
Servings: 4
Ingredients:

- Two scallions, cut into pieces
- ¾ cup packed fresh flat-leaf parsley
- ¼ cup packed fresh basil leaves
- 1 teaspoon lemon zest
- 3 tablespoons fresh lemon juice
- 1 tablespoon olive oil
- 20 sea scallops
- Two teaspoons of butter, melted
- Pinch salt
- ⅛ teaspoon lemon pepper

Directions:

1. Prepare and preheat the grill to medium-high. Make sure the grill rack is clean.

2. Meanwhile, make the gremolata. In a blender or food processor, mix the scallions, parsley, basil, lemon zest, lemon juice, and olive oil. Blend or process until the herbs are finely chopped. Pour into a small bowl and set aside.

3. Put the scallops on a plate. If the scallops have a small tough muscle attached to them, remove and discard it. Brush the melted butter over the scallops. Sprinkle with salt and lemon pepper.

4. Place the scallops in a grill basket if you have one. If not, place a sheet of heavy-duty foil on the grill, punch some holes in it, and arrange the scallops evenly across it.

5. Grill the scallops for 2 to 3 minutes per side, turning once, until opaque. Drizzle with the gremolata and serve.

Per serving: Calories: 190kcal; Fat: 7g; Carbs: 2g; Protein: 28g; Saturated Fat: 2g; Cholesterol: 68mg; Sugar: 1g

24. Salmon Patties

Difficulty: ★★★☆☆
Preparation time: 20 minutes
Cooking time: 40 minutes
Servings: 4
Ingredients:

- ¼ cup quinoa, rinsed
- ½ cup water
- 2 (7½-ounce) cans of low-sodium deboned salmon, packed in water
- 1 tablespoon mustard
- One teaspoon of Old Bay Seasoning
- 2 large eggs
- olive oil

Directions:

1. In a saucepan over high heat, mix the quinoa and water and bring to a boil. Reduce the heat to low, and simmer until the liquid is absorbed about 20 minutes. Remove from the heat, fluff with a fork, and let cool.

2. Preheat the oven to 400°F. Line a baking sheet with parchment paper.

3. Mix the salmon, mustard, and seasoning in a huge bowl until well combined.

4. Add the quinoa and eggs and combine well, then shape the mixture into five patties.

5. Place the patties on the prepared baking sheet and bake for 20 minutes until they are slightly brown on the edges. Serve hot.

Per serving: Calories: 202kcal; Fat: 10g; Carbs: 6g; Protein: 23g; Saturated Fat: 2g; Cholesterol: 34mg; Sugar: 4g

25. Farfalle With Asparagus And Smoked Salmon

Difficulty: ★★★★☆
Preparation time: 10 minutes
Cooking time: 2 hours 20 minutes
Servings: 4
Ingredients:

- 1 (8 oz.) package of farfalle pasta
- 1/2 cup fresh steamed asparagus tips
- 1 oz. smoked salmon, chopped
- 1 lemon, juiced
- 1 tbsp. chopped pistachio nuts
- 1 tsp. chopped fresh basil
- 1 tbsp. extra virgin olive oil
- salt and pepper to taste

Directions:

1. Cook the pasta in salted boiling water in a huge pot. Use cold water to rinse, then drain.

2. Steam asparagus over boiling water until it gets softened yet still firm. Drain well, let it cool and chop.

3. Mix pepper, salt, olive oil, basil, pistachios, lemon juice, smoked salmon, asparagus and pasta in a large bowl. Combine well and put into the refrigerator for 2 hours. Take it out, and serve it at room temperature.

Per serving: Calories: 261kcal; Fat: 6g; Carbs: 45g; Protein: 10g; Saturated Fat: 2g; Cholesterol: 2mg; Sugar: 1g

26. Cod With Italian Crumb Topping

Difficulty: ★★☆☆☆

Preparation time: 15 minutes

Cooking time: 10 minutes

Servings: 4

Ingredients:

- 1/4 cup fine dry bread crumbs
- 2 tbsps. grated Parmesan cheese
- 1 tbsp. cornmeal
- 1 tsp. olive oil
- 1/2 tsp. Italian seasoning
- 1/8 tsp. garlic powder
- 1/8 tsp. ground black pepper
- 4 (3 oz.) fillets cod fillets
- One egg white, lightly beaten

Directions:

1. Preheat the oven to 450 degrees Fahrenheit.
2. Mix pepper, garlic powder, Italian seasoning, oil, cornmeal, cheese, and breadcrumbs in a small shallow bowl.
3. Use cooking spray to cover the rack of a boiling pan. Add the cod into the rack, folding under any thin edges of the filets. Use the egg white to brush, then scoop the crumb mixture over.
4. Bake in a preheated oven till opaque throughout, and fish can be flaked easily with a fork for 10 to 12 minutes.

Per serving: Calories: 131kcal; Fat: 3g; Carbs: 7g; Protein: 18g; Saturated Fat: 1g; Cholesterol: 39mg; Sugar: 2g

CHAPTER 3: Poultry

27. Sweet Salad Dressing Chicken and Carrot Sheet Pan Dinner

Difficulty: ★★★☆☆

Preparation time: 5 minutes + 30 minutes to marinate

Cooking time: 25 minutes

Servings: 4

Ingredients:

- 1-pound boneless, skinless chicken thighs
- ½ cup Sweet Salad Dressing
- 2½ cups carrots cut into thin matchsticks
- 1½ tablespoons olive oil
- One tablespoon of minced garlic
- Sea salt
- Freshly ground black pepper

Directions:

1. Place the chicken and Sweet Salad Dressing in a resealable plastic bag and marinate for 30 minutes or overnight in the refrigerator.
2. Preheat the oven to 425°F. Line a baking sheet with parchment.
3. In a bowl, toss the carrots with olive oil and garlic, season with salt and pepper, and set aside.
4. Place the chicken on half of the prepared baking sheet and bake for 25 minutes until it reaches an internal temperature of 165°F.
5. After 5 minutes, add the carrots to the other side of the baking sheet and bake them with the chicken for the remaining 20 minutes, flipping the carrots halfway through. Enjoy immediately.

Per serving: Calories: 213kcal; Fat: 8g; Carbs: 17g; Protein: 19g; Saturated Fat: 2g; Cholesterol: 2mg; Sugar: 5g

28. Piña Colada Chicken

Difficulty: ★★★☆☆

Preparation time: 5 minutes

Cooking time: 20 minutes

Servings: 2

Ingredients:

- Aluminum foil
- 2 (4 oz) chicken breasts, pounded flat
- 2 tsp unsweetened coconut flakes
- 1 (20 oz) can of crushed pineapple, drained
- 1 cup green bell peppers, diced
- ¼ cup soy sauce

Directions:

1. Heat the oven to 400°F gas mark 6. Line a baking sheet with aluminum foil.
2. Place the chicken breasts on the baking sheet and top with coconut flakes.
3. Place the pineapple and green bell peppers around the chicken breasts.
4. Drizzle the chicken breasts with soy sauce and cook for 10 to 15 minutes until the pineapple is caramelized and the chicken is cooked. Serve warm.

Per serving: Calories: 327kcal; Fat: 6g; Carbs: 23g; Protein: 31g; Saturated Fat: 1g; Cholesterol: 80mg; Sugar: 3g

29. Grilled Chicken Salad With Olives And Oranges

Difficulty: ★★★☆☆

Preparation time: 10 minutes

Cooking time: 10 minutes

Servings: 4

Ingredients:

For the dressing:

- 4 minced garlic cloves,

- 1/2 cup of red wine vinegar
- Cracked black pepper; to taste.
- 1 tablespoon of extra-virgin olive oil
- One tablespoon of finely chopped celery.
- One tablespoon of finely chopped red onion.

For the salad:

- 2 garlic cloves
- 4 skinless, boneless chicken breasts, 4 ounce
- 8 cups of washed and dried leaf lettuce,
- Two navels peeled and sliced oranges,
- 16 ripe large (black) olives

Directions:

1. Mix the garlic, vinegar, olive oil, celery, onion, and pepper in a small bowl to prepare the dressing. Stir to ensure that everything is equally distributed. Cover and keep refrigerated until ready to use.
2. Build a fire/heat a broiler or gas grill in a charcoal grill. Spray the grill rack or broiler pan gently with cooking spray away from the heat source. Put the rack 4 to 6 inches away from the heat source. Garlic cloves should be rubbed into the chicken breasts and then discarded. For 5 minutes, broil the chicken on each side until browned and cooked through. Allow five mins for the chicken to rest on a chopping board before slicing it into strips.
3. Two cups of lettuce, 1/4 of the sliced oranges, and four olives are placed on four plates. Drizzle dressing over each dish and top with one chicken breast sliced into strips. Serve right away.

Per serving: Calories: 237kcal; Fat: 9g; Carbs: 12g; Protein: 27g; Saturated Fat: 2g; Cholesterol: 49mg; Sugar: 3g

30. Lime Chicken Wraps

Difficulty: ★☆☆☆☆
Preparation time: 5 minutes
Cooking time: 0 minutes
Servings: 2
Ingredients:

- 1 cup chicken breasts, cooked and chopped
- 1 cup low-sodium canned kidney beans, rinsed and drained
- ½ ripe avocado, diced
- One spring onion, finely chopped
- ½ lime, juiced and zested
- 1 tsp parsley, finely chopped
- ¼ tsp ground cumin
- Four large iceberg lettuce leaves

Directions:

1. In a medium-sized mixing bowl, add the chicken breasts, kidney beans, avocado, spring onion, lime juice and zest, parsley, and d cumin until well combined.
2. Divide the chicken filling evenly between the lettuce leaves and roll closed.
3. Serve cold.

Per serving: Calories: 368kcal; Fat: 11g; Carbs: 40g; Protein: 30g; Saturated Fat: 2g; Cholesterol: 53mg; Sugar: 1g

31. Spicy Honey Chicken And Eggplant

Difficulty: ★★★☆☆
Preparation time: 10 minutes, plus 30 minutes to marinate
Cooking time: 30 minutes
Servings: 4
Ingredients:

- 1 pound boneless, skinless chicken thighs
- ⅓ cup Spicy Honey Sauce

- 2 eggplants, cut into ¼-inch-thick slices
- 2 tablespoons minced garlic
- Sea salt
- Freshly ground black pepper

Directions:

1. Place the chicken and the Spicy Honey Sauce in a resealable plastic bag, and marinate in the refrigerator for 30 minutes or overnight.
2. Preheat the oven to 400°F. Line a baking sheet with parchment paper.
3. Place the eggplant slices on half of the prepared baking sheet, sprinkle them with the garlic, and season them with salt and pepper.
4. Spread out the chicken on the other half of the baking sheet.
5. Cook until the eggplant is caramelized and the chicken reaches an internal temperature of 165°F, about 25 to 30 minutes. Serve immediately.

Per serving: Calories: 248kcal; Fat: 10g; Carbs: 21g; Protein: 20g; Saturated Fat: 1g; Cholesterol: 36mg; Sugar: 6g

32. Chicken Curry

Difficulty: ★★☆☆☆
Preparation time: 5 minutes
Cooking time: 15 minutes
Servings: 4
Ingredients:

- 1 tablespoon olive oil
- 1 lb boneless, skinless chicken thighs, thinly sliced
- One tablespoon of minced garlic
- 1 white onion, diced
- 2 tablespoons curry powder
- ½ cup fat-free plain Greek yogurt
- Pinch sea salt

Directions:

1. In a skillet over medium heat, heat the olive oil and cook the chicken and garlic

until the chicken is cooked through about 10 minutes.
2. Add the onion and cook until it is translucent about 5 minutes.
3. Add the curry powder and stir for 1 to 2 minutes until it is fragrant.
4. Take the skillet from the heat, stir in the yogurt, and season with a pinch of salt. Serve immediately.

Per serving: Calories: 160kcal; Fat: 7g; Carbs: 4g; Protein: 20g; Saturated Fat: 1g; Cholesterol: 15mg; Sugar: 7g

33. Chicken, Mushroom, And Bell Pepper Skewers

Difficulty: ★★☆☆☆
Preparation time: 10 minutes
Cooking time: 17 minutes
Servings: 4
Ingredients:

- 1 lb skinless, boneless chicken breast (skinless), cut into 1-inch cubes
- ⅓ cup Oregano-Thyme Sauce
- Two bell peppers, cut into 1-inch chunks
- 24 whole white mushrooms
- One tablespoon of minced garlic
- 1½ tablespoons olive oil
- Sea salt

Directions:

1. Preheat the oven to 450°F. Line a baking sheet with parchment paper.
2. In a medium bowl, toss the chicken breast with the Oregano-Thyme Sauce.
3. In another medium bowl, toss the peppers and mushrooms with garlic, olive oil, and a pinch of salt.
4. Thread the chicken, peppers, and mushrooms onto eight wooden or metal skewers. (If using wooden skewers, be sure to soak them for 30 minutes beforehand.)
5. Bring the skewers on the prepared baking sheet and bake for about 17

minutes, until the chicken edges are slightly brown and cooked to an internal temperature of 165°F. Serve immediately.

Per serving: Calories: 191kcal; Fat: 7g; Carbs: 8g; Protein: 24g; Saturated Fat: 1g; Cholesterol: 12mg; Sugar: 3g

34. Cashew Chicken

Difficulty: ★★☆☆☆
Preparation time: 5 minutes
Cooking time: 5 minutes
Servings: 2
Ingredients:

- 2 tsp olive oil
- 2 tsp garlic, minced, divided
- ½ cup red onion, chopped
- 8 oz ground chicken
- 1 tsp ginger, grated
- 3 tbsp. unsalted cashew butter
- 4 tbsp. water
- Six large green leaf lettuce leaves
- ½ cup unsalted cashew nuts, roughly chopped

Directions:

1. Preheat the olive oil in a frying pan over medium heat. Add the 1 tsp garlic and onion, and cook for 1 to 2 minutes, until translucent.
2. Add the chicken and separate using a fork. Continue mixing for 5 minutes until lightly golden and cooked through.
3. Add the ginger, remaining 1 tsp garlic, cashew butter, and water to combine in a small mixing bowl.
4. Add the cashew mixture to the ground chicken. Cook for 1 minute until all flavors have combined.
5. Divide the cashew chicken mixture into the lettuce cups and serve topped with the cashew nuts.

Per serving: Calories: 414kcal; Fat: 21g; Carbs: 17g; Protein: 32g; Saturated Fat: 4g; Cholesterol: 90mg; Sugar: 5g

35. Red Wine Chicken

Difficulty: ★★★☆☆
Preparation time: 5 minutes
Cooking time: 30 minutes
Servings: 4
Ingredients:

- 2 tbsp. plant-based butter, plus 1 tbsp. olive oil
- One lb. boneless, skinless chicken thighs
- ¼ tsp fine sea salt
- Ground black pepper
- 3 large carrots, peeled and thinly sliced
- 8 oz button mushrooms, sliced
- 1 small brown onion, sliced
- 1 cup Pinot Noir red wine
- 1 cup low-sodium chicken stock
- 1 tbsp. tomato paste
- 3 rosemary sprigs

Directions:

1. Melt the butter in a huge, heavy-bottom pan over medium-high heat. Sprinkle the chicken thighs with salt and pepper.
2. Once the butter starts to froth, add the chicken thighs, and brown for 1 to 2 minutes on each side. Transfer to a plate.
3. Add the carrots, mushrooms, and onion to the pan. Fry for 3-4 minutes 'til the onion starts to soften. Add the red wine, chicken stock, tomato paste, and rosemary sprigs. Cook for 7 to 8 minutes, 'til the vegetables are tender.
4. Return the chicken thighs to the pan, and simmer for 5 to 10 minutes until cooked through. Remove the rosemary sprigs and serve.

Per serving: Calories: 296kcal; Fat: 12g; Carbs: 11g; Protein: 26g; Saturated Fat: 3g; Cholesterol: 115mg; Sugar: 9g

36. Chicken Rice

Difficulty: ★★☆☆☆
Preparation time: 15 minutes
Cooking time: 15 minutes
Servings: 3
Ingredients:

- 1 cup brown basmati rice, cooked
- 1 cup chicken breast, cooked and chopped
- 1 cup spinach, cooked and shredded
- ½ cup low-sodium canned garbanzo beans drained and rinsed
- 4 tbsp. lemon and herb vinaigrette, divided
- 1 large carrot, peeled and grated
- 1 large red bell pepper, diced
- 1 large green bell pepper, diced
- 1 cup frozen peas, cooked
- ½ cup frozen corn, cooked
- ¼ cup pine nuts, toasted for garnish

Directions:

1. Add the basmati rice, chicken breasts, spinach, garbanzo beans, and 2 tbsp in a medium-sized mixing bowl. of the lemon and herb vinaigrette, mix to combine.
2. Divide the rice mixture between two large bowls, arrange the carrot, red bell pepper, green bell pepper, peas, and corn in the bowls, and drizzle with the remaining lemon and herb vinaigrette.
3. Top with pine nuts and serve.

Per serving: Calories: 503kcal; Fat: 21g; Carbs: 53g; Protein: 32g; Saturated Fat: 3g; Cholesterol: 54mg; Sugar: 8g

37. Lemon Chicken And Asparagus

Difficulty: ★★★☆☆
Preparation time: 10 minutes + 30 minutes to marinate
Cooking time: 20 minutes
Servings: 4
Ingredients:

- 1 lb boneless, skinless chicken thighs (skinless), cut into 1-inch pieces
- ½ cup Lemon-Garlic Sauce
- 2½ cups (about 1 pound) chopped asparagus
- One tablespoon of minced garlic
- 1½ tablespoons olive oil
- Sea salt
- Freshly ground black pepper

Directions:

1. Place the chicken and Lemon-Garlic Sauce in a resealable plastic bag and marinate in the refrigerator for 30 minutes or overnight.
2. In a bowl, toss the asparagus with the garlic and olive oil, and season with salt and pepper.
3. In a large skillet over high heat, sauté the chicken until cooked and browned, about 15 minutes. Transfer the chicken with a slotted spoon to a plate and set aside.
4. Add the asparagus to the skillet and sauté until tender-crisp, about 5 minutes. Enjoy immediately.

Per serving: Calories: 221kcal; Fat: 13g; Carbs: 6g; Protein: 20g; Saturated Fat: 3g; Cholesterol: 0mg; Sugar: 5g

38. Mediterranean Patties

Difficulty: ★★★☆☆
Preparation time: 15 minutes
Cooking time: 15 minutes
Servings: 4
Ingredients:

- Aluminium foil
- 1 cup broccoli florets
- 1 small red onion, quartered
- ¼ cup black olives pitted
- 8 oz baby spinach, roughly chopped

- 1 lb. ground chicken
- 1½ tsp. Mediterranean seasoning rub blend
- 4 whole wheat buns
- lettuce
- tomato

Directions:

1. Preheat the oven to broil. Line a baking sheet with aluminum foil.
2. In a food processor, pulse the broccoli, onion, and olives for 1 to 2 minutes until minced.
3. In a large-sized mixing bowl, add the baby spinach, broccoli mixture, chicken, and the Mediterranean spice blend, and mix to combine. Form into eight medium-sized patties and place them on the baking sheet.
4. Broil for 10 mins on one side, flip, then broil for 3 mins on the other until golden brown.
5. Serve on whole wheat buns with lettuce and tomato or with a garden salad.

Per serving: Calories: 206kcal; Fat: 10g; Carbs: 7g; Protein: 25g; Saturated Fat: 3g; Cholesterol: 84mg; Sugar: 5g

39. Iron Packed Turkey

Difficulty: ★★★☆☆
Preparation time: 5 minutes
Cooking time: 30 minutes
Servings: 2
Ingredients:

- 2 (3 oz) turkey breasts, boneless and skinless
- Himalayan pink salt
- Ground black pepper
- 3 tsp avocado oil, divided
- 1 ½ cups spinach, roughly chopped
- 1 ½ cups kale, roughly chopped
- 1 ½ cups Swiss chard, roughly chopped
- 1 ½ cups collard greens, roughly chopped
- 1 tsp garlic crushed

Directions:

1. Preheat the oven to 400°F gas mark 6.
2. Season the turkey breasts with salt and pepper to taste.
3. Heat 1 tsp of avocado oil in a large cast-iron frying pan over medium-high heat.
4. Add the turkey breasts and cook for 5 minutes on each side until browned. Remove the turkey breasts and set them aside.
5. Add the remaining 2 tsp of avocado oil to the pan and fry the spinach, kale, Swiss chard, collard greens and garlic for 3 minutes until they are slightly wilted.
6. Season the mixed greens with salt and pepper to taste, and place the turkey breasts on the greens.
7. Place the cast iron frying pan in the oven and bake for 15 minutes until the turkey breasts are cooked.
8. Serve warm.

Per serving: Calories: 113kcal; Fat: 2g; Carbs: 4g; Protein: 22g; Saturated Fat: 0g; Cholesterol: 49mg; Sugar: 2g

40. Lime Turkey Skewers

Difficulty: ★★★☆☆
Preparation time: 5 minutes
Cooking time: 15 minutes
Servings: 4
Ingredients:

- One lb. boneless, skinless turkey breasts, cut into chunks
- 1 lime, juiced
- 2 tbsp. avocado oil, plus 1 tbsp.
- 2 tbsp. garlic, minced
- 1 tsp dried thyme
- 1 tsp dried dill

- ½ tsp fine sea salt
- ¼ tsp ground black pepper

Directions:

1. Add the turkey breasts, lime juice, avocado oil, garlic, thyme, dill, salt and pepper to a medium-sized mixing bowl. Rest for 30 minutes in the fridge.
2. Thread the marinated turkey chunks onto eight skewers.
3. Heat 1 tbsp. of avocado oil in a heavy-bottom pan over medium-high heat.
4. Place the skewers gently in the pan, fry for 5 to 7 minutes, flip, and cook for 5 to 8 minutes, or until the turkey is cooked and no longer pink inside. Remove from the heat and serve.

Per serving: Calories: 205kcal; Fat: 10g; Carbs: 2g; Protein: 26g; Saturated Fat: 3g; Cholesterol: 26mg; Sugar: 7g

41. Italian Chicken Bake

Difficulty: ★★★☆☆
Preparation time: 5 minutes
Cooking time: 25 minutes
Servings: 4
Ingredients:

- One lb. chicken breasts halved lengthwise into four pieces
- ½ tsp garlic powder
- ½ tsp fine sea salt
- ¼ tsp ground black pepper
- ¼ tsp Italian seasoning
- ½ cup basil, finely chopped
- 4 part-skim mozzarella cheese slices
- Two large Roma tomatoes, finely chopped

Directions:

1. Heat the oven to 400°F gas mark 6.
2. Season the cut chicken breasts with garlic powder, salt, pepper and Italian seasoning.

3. Place the seasoned chicken breasts on a baking sheet. Bake for 18 to 22 minutes until the chicken breasts are cooked through. Remove from the oven and set it to broil on high.
4. Evenly place the basil, one mozzarella slice and tomatoes on each chicken breast.
5. Return the baking sheet to the oven, then broil for 2 to 3 minutes, until the cheese has melted and browned.
6. Remove from the oven and serve hot.

Per serving: Calories: 239kcal; Fat: 9g; Carbs: 4g; Protein: 33g; Saturated Fat: 4g; Cholesterol: 15mg; Sugar: 8g

42. One Pan Chicken

Difficulty: ★★★☆☆
Preparation time: 5 minutes
Cooking time: 30 minutes
Servings: 4
Ingredients:

- 2 tbsp. olive oil
- Four bone-in chicken thighs, skin removed
- ¾ tsp Himalayan pink salt, divided
- ½ tsp ground black pepper, divided
- 1 (15 ounces) can of petite diced tomatoes, drained
- ¼ cup water
- 1 (14 oz) can asparagus cut spears, drained
- ¼ cup black olives pitted
- ¼ cup cilantro, chopped

Directions:

1. Heat the oven to 350°F gas mark 4.
2. Heat the olive oil in a large oven-proof frying pan over medium-high heat.
3. Season the chicken thighs with ¼ tsp of salt and ¼ tsp of pepper. Place the thighs in the frying pan and cook for 2 to

3 minutes per side, or until lightly browned; transfer to a plate.

4. Add the drained tomatoes and water and deglaze in the same pan by scraping the bottom bits from the pan.

5. Add the asparagus, black olives, ½ tsp salt and ¼ tsp pepper, and combine.

6. Bring the chicken thighs back into the pan and push them down into the tomato mixture.

7. Place the ovenproof pan in the oven and bake for 20 minutes until the chicken is fully cooked.

8. Remove from the oven and sprinkle with cilantro; serve warm.

Per serving: Calories: 270kcal; Fat: 13g; Carbs: 15g; Protein: 26g; Saturated Fat: 2g; Cholesterol: 62mg; Sugar: 3g

43. Turkey Oat Patties

Difficulty: ★★★☆☆
Preparation time: 5 minutes
Cooking time: 30 minutes
Servings: 6
Ingredients:

- Aluminum foil
- 1 lb. lean ground turkey
- ½ cup rolled oats
- ¼ cup sun-dried tomatoes julienne cut, drained
- ¼ cup brown onion, finely chopped
- ¼ cup parsley, finely chopped
- 1 tbsp. garlic, crushed
- Six whole-wheat hamburger buns
- 1 ripe avocado, peeled, pitted, and mashed
- 6 iceberg lettuce leaves
- 6 Roma tomato slices
- Hamburger dill pickle chips

Directions:

1. Preheat the oven to broil. Line a baking sheet with aluminum foil.

2. Add the turkey, oats, sun-dried tomatoes, onion, parsley, and garlic to combine in a large mixing bowl. Shape into six patties.

3. Place the turkey patties on the baking sheet, and broil for 3 to 4 minutes on each side until fully cooked and the juices clear.

4. Meanwhile, prepare a self-serving platter with the buns, mashed avocado, lettuce leaves, tomato slices, and dill pickle chips. Assemble the way you like.

Per serving: Calories: 366kcal; Fat: 15g; Carbs: 35g; Protein: 24g; Saturated Fat: 3g; Cholesterol: 35mg; Sugar: 6g

44. Balsamic Blueberry Chicken

Difficulty: ★★★☆☆
Preparation time: 5 minutes
Cooking time: 25 minutes
Servings: 2
Ingredients:

- Aluminum foil
- ½ cup fresh blueberries
- 2 tbsp. pine nuts
- ¼ cup cilantro, chopped
- 2 tbsp. balsamic vinegar
- ¼ tsp ground black pepper
- 2 (4 oz) chicken breasts, butterflied

Directions:

1. Heat the oven to 375 deg. F gas mark 5. Line a baking sheet with aluminum foil.

2. In a medium-sized mixing bowl, add the blueberries, pine nuts, cilantro, balsamic vinegar, and pepper until well combined.

3. Place the chicken breasts on the baking sheet and pour the blueberry mixture on top.

4. Bake for 20-25 minutes 'til the juices are caramelized and the inside of the chicken has cooked through. Serve warm.

Per serving: Calories: 212kcal; Fat: 7g; Carbs: 11g; Protein: 27g; Saturated Fat: 1g; Cholesterol: 80mg; Sugar: 1g

CHAPTER 4: Meat

45. Flank Steak With Caramelized Onions

Difficulty: ★★★★☆
Preparation time: 10 minutes
Cooking time: 30 minutes
Servings: 4
Ingredients:

- Two large thinly sliced and halved lengthwise red onions,
- 1 tablespoon of butter
- 1/2 teaspoon of dried sage
- One green or red bell pepper; thin strips
- 11 -1/4 to 1 1/2 pounds, beef flank steak
- 1/2 teaspoon of dried oregano
- One tablespoon of black pepper; freshly ground.
- 1/2 teaspoon of salt
- One 15-ounce can of black beans rinsed and drained, warmed.
- 4 7- to 8-inch warmed flour tortillas

Directions:

1. In a huge pan over medium heat, melt the butter. Cover and simmer onions, occasionally turning, until they are soft, for approximately 7 minutes. Add sage, bell pepper strips, and oregano.
2. Cook, uncovered, over medium-high heat for 4 to 5 minutes, or until the peppers are crisp-tender and the onions are golden, stirring frequently. Preheat the grill pan to medium-high temperature.
3. Trim the fat off the steak and score it on both sides with shallow diamond cuts at 1-inch intervals—season with salt and pepper. Grill, rotating once, for 8 to 12 minutes for the medium-rare or 12 to 15 minutes for the medium. Thinly slice steak across the grain diagonally and

cover it with an onion mixture. Warm the tortillas, and black beans are served on the side.

Per serving: Calories: 434kcal; Fat: 15g; Carbs: 36g; Protein: 40g; Saturated Fat: 3g; Cholesterol: 37mg; Sugar: 7g

46. Juicy Burgers

Difficulty: ★★★☆☆
Preparation time: 10 minutes
Cooking time: 10 minutes
Servings: 5
Ingredients:

- 1 cup low sodium beef broth
- Two slices of white bread, torn into pieces
- 1 1/2 pounds extra-lean ground beef (93% lean)
- Two tablespoons of egg substitute
- 1/2 teaspoon black pepper

Directions:

1. Microwave broth in a glass bowl for 30 seconds. Add bread pieces and combine with your hands.
2. Combine broth mixture and remaining ingredients. Shape into five patties—grill patties over medium-high heat for 6 to 8 minutes on each side or to desired doneness.

Per serving: Calories: 328kcal; Fat: 9g; Carbs: 0g; Protein: 27g; Saturated Fat: 3g; Cholesterol: 94mg; Sugar: 2g

47. Steak And Vegetables With Chimichurri Sauce

Difficulty: ★★★★☆
Preparation time: 20 minutes
Cooking time: 40 minutes
Servings: 4
Ingredients:

Steak & Vegetables

- ½ teaspoon of chili powder
- 1 pound of top sirloin beef steak; boneless, 1 inch thick
- ¼ teaspoon of salt
- One small red onion, 1/2-inch-thick slices
- 2 cups of cherry tomatoes or grape tomatoes
- Nonstick cooking spray
- Two medium-trimmed zucchini or yellow summer squash halved lengthwise.

Chimichurri Sauce

- ½ cup of fresh cilantro; lightly packed
- 1 cup of fresh, lightly packed flat-leaf parsley
- ¼ cup of white wine vinegar
- 1 tablespoon of olive oil
- 2 tablespoons of water
- ¼ teaspoon of salt
- Six minced cloves of garlic,
- ¼ teaspoon of crushed red pepper (Optional)
- ¼ teaspoon of ground black pepper

Directions:

1. Trim the fat off the steak. Use a knife to cut the meat into four equal pieces. Season the steak pieces with 1/8 teaspoon of salt and chili powder. Using four 6- to 8-inch skewers, thread tomatoes onto the skewers. Lightly brush the zucchini, tomatoes, and red onion slices on both sides with nonstick spray. Sprinkle the remaining 1/8 tsp of salt into the veggies.

2. Place tomato skewers, steak, and vegetable slices on the uncovered grill rack directly over medium embers using a charcoal grill. Grill the steak 'til it reaches your preferred level of doneness, flipping once halfway through. Allow it 14 to 18 minutes for the medium-rare doneness (145 degrees Fahrenheit) or 18 to 22 minutes for the medium doneness (145 degrees Fahrenheit) to (160 degrees F). Grill onion slices and zucchini for 10 to 12 minutes, turning periodically, until soft and faintly browned in spots. Grill the tomatoes for 4 to 6 minutes, rotating once or until softened and faintly browned. (Preheat the grill if using a gas grill.) Reduce to a medium heat setting. Place the tomato skewers, steak, and vegetable slices on the grill rack and cook them over high heat. Cover and cook as directed above).

3. Chimichurri Sauce Preparation: In a blender or food processor, combine cilantro, parsley, vinegar, olive oil, water, garlic, ground black pepper, salt, and, if preferred, crushed red pepper. Cover and mix or pulse occasionally on/off until chopped but not pureed. Using four serving dishes, divide the sliced meat. Grilled tomatoes, Chimichurri sauce, and veggie pieces are served on the side.

Per serving: Calories: 245kcal; Fat: 8g; Carbs: 13g; Protein: 28g; Saturated Fat: 2g; Cholesterol: 47mg; Sugar: 3g

48. Bbq Pulled Pork With Greek Yogurt Slaw

Difficulty: ★★★★☆
Preparation time: 10 minutes
Cooking time: 1 hour
Servings: 4
Ingredients:

- 3 cups of green cabbage; shredded
- 1/2 cup of non-fat plain greek yogurt
- 3 cups of red cabbage; shredded
- 1 (12oz.) can of diet root beer
- 2 tsp of lemon juice

- 1 tbsp. of apple cider vinegar
- 1/4 tsp of celery salt
- 1 tsp of Dijon mustard
- One can of light cooking spray
- 1 1/2 lbs. pork tenderloin; halved
- 1 pinch stevia
- Four sachets of buttermilk cheddar herb biscuit
- 1/2 cup of BBQ sauce; sugar-free

Directions:

1. Cooking spray is used to coat the interior of the Instant Pot. On a high sauté ' setting, brown the pork chunks on all sides for approximately 3 minutes.

2. Close the pressure valve after adding the diet root beer. Set the timer for 60 minutes on high. Allow for natural pressure release before opening. Prepare the slaw in the meanwhile. Combine cabbage, yogurt, apple cider vinegar, lemon juice, Dijon mustard, salt, and stevia in a medium-sized mixing bowl.

3. Remove the pork from the Instant Pot and shred it in a bowl. Toss in the barbecue sauce and mix well. Bake Herb Biscuits according to package instructions, if desired. Serve the slaw and shredded pork on the biscuits or without baked biscuits.

Per serving: Calories: 108kcal; Fat: 3g; Carbs: 14g; Protein: 6g; Saturated Fat: 1g; Cholesterol: 40mg; Sugar: 2g

49. Mexican Stuffed Peppers With Corn And Black Beans

Difficulty: ★★★☆☆
Preparation time: 10 minutes
Cooking time: 30 minutes
Servings: 6
Ingredients:

- Six bell peppers; any colour
- 1 tablespoon of olive oil
- 1 chopped yellow onion,
- 2 minced cloves of garlic,
- 1 pound of lean ground beef
- 1 tablespoon of chili powder
- 1 1/2 teaspoons of ground cumin
- 1 (4-ounce) can of diced green chiles
- 1 1/2 cups of cooked white rice
- 2 medium diced tomatoes,
- 1 (15-ounce) can have drained and rinsed black beans,
- 1 cup of defrosted frozen corn,
- 1/2 cup of shredded Cheddar cheese or Mexican-blend
- Optional toppings: Chopped fresh cilantro or green onions.

Directions:

1. Preheat the oven to 350 degrees Fahrenheit. A big pot of water is brought to a boil. Slice the peppers vertically through the center of the stem and to the bottom. Remove the membranes as well as the seeds.

2. For 3–4 minutes, until the peppers are somewhat softened, parboil them in a saucepan of water. Drain the peppers and arrange them cut side up in a wide baking dish. Warm the oil in a wide skillet over medium heat. Sauté for 4 minutes or until the onion is transparent—cook for another minute after adding the garlic.

3. Cook for 5 minutes, or until the ground beef is brown, frequently stirring to break up the meat. Chili powder, green chiles, cooked rice, black beans, tomatoes, cumin, and maize are added—season with pepper and salt to taste. Fill the peppers halfway with the ground beef rice mixture and top with cheese. Bake for 15-20 minutes, until the peppers are soft and the cheese has melted. If using, garnish with cilantro or green onions and serve warm.

Per serving: Calories: 357kcal; Fat: 7g; Carbs: 46g; Protein: 26g; Saturated Fat: 2g; Cholesterol: 46mg; Sugar: 8g

50. Meatloaf

Difficulty: ★★★★☆
Preparation time: 10 minutes
Cooking time: 1- 1 ½ hour
Servings: 6
Ingredients:

- 1 1/2 pounds extra-lean ground beef (93% lean)
- 1 cup bread crumbs
- 1 onion, finely chopped
- 1/4 cup egg substitute
- 1/4 teaspoon black pepper
- 8 ounces of no-salt-added tomato sauce, divided
- 1/2 cup water
- Two teaspoons of Worcestershire sauce
- 3 tablespoons vinegar
- 2 tablespoons mustard
- 3 tablespoons brown sugar

Directions:

1. Preheat oven to 350 deg. F (gas mark 4). Mix beef, breadcrumbs, onion, egg substitute, pepper, and half the tomato sauce.
2. Form into one large loaf or two small ones; mix remaining tomato sauce and ingredients together; pour over loaves— bake for 1 to 1 1/2 hours.

Per serving: Calories: 393kcal; Fat: 9g; Carbs: 23g; Protein: 26g; Saturated Fat: 3g; Cholesterol: 78mg; Sugar: 3g

51. Oaxacan Tacos

Difficulty: ★★★☆☆
Preparation time: 10 minutes
Cooking time: 15 minutes
Servings: 9

Ingredients:

- ground black pepper and salt to taste
- 2 pounds of top sirloin steak, thin strips
- 4 limes, wedges
- ¼ cup of vegetable oil
- 1 diced onion,
- 18 corn tortillas; (6 inches)
- One bunch of fresh cilantro; chopped,
- Four fresh seeded and chopped jalapeno peppers

Directions:

1. In a huge skillet, heat the oil over medium-high heat. Put meat in the tit and cook for 5 minutes in a hot pan until the steak is browned on the outer side and cooked. Sprinkle salt & pepper to taste.
2. Place on a platter to keep warm. In the same skillet, heat the oil. Put the tortilla in the heated oil and cook until lightly browned and pliable, flipping once. Continue with the remaining tortillas. On a platter, arrange tortillas and top with steak, jalapeño, onion, and cilantro. Lime juice should be squeezed over the top.

Per serving: Calories: 379kcal; Fat: 21g; Carbs: 28g; Protein: 20g; Saturated Fat: 4g; Cholesterol: 58mg; Sugar: 6g

52. Mexican Skillet Meal

Difficulty: ★★★☆☆
Preparation time: 5 minutes
Cooking time: 30 minutes
Servings: 5
Ingredients:

- 1-pound extra-lean ground beef (93% lean)
- 1/2 cup onion, chopped
- 1/4 cup green bell peppers, chopped
- 1/4 cup red bell pepper, chopped
- 1/2 teaspoon minced garlic
- 1 1/2 cups rice
- 3 cups water
- Two teaspoons of low sodium beef bouillon
- 2 cups canned no-salt-added tomatoes
- 1 tablespoon chili powder
- 1/2 teaspoon cumin
- 1/4 teaspoon dried oregano
- 1 2 ounces frozen corn, thawed

Directions:

1. Sauté beef, onion, green and red bell peppers, and garlic in a large skillet until beef is browned and vegetables are tender.
2. Add rice and sauté 2 minutes longer. Stir in the remaining ingredients. Bring to boil. Reduce heat, cover, and simmer for 20 minutes, until rice is tender and liquid absorbed.

Per serving: Calories: 357kcal; Fat: 7g; Carbs: 33g; Protein: 22g; Saturated Fat: 2g; Cholesterol: 63mg; Sugar: 4g

53. Tailgate Chili

Difficulty: ★★★★☆
Preparation time: 5 minutes
Cooking time: 35 minutes
Servings: 4
Ingredients:

- 1 medium chopped onion
- One lb. ground beef; 95% lean
- One medium chopped jalapeño
- One medium green chopped bell pepper
- 1 Tbsp. of chili powder
- Four cloves of fresh garlic; minced, OR 2 tsp. of jarred minced garlic.
- 1/2 tsp. of ground coriander
- 1 Tbsp. of ground cumin
- 15.5 oz. canned, low-sodium, or no-salt-added pinto/kidney beans, rinsed and drained.
- 3/4 cup of jarred salsa (low sodium)
- 14.5 oz. of canned, low-sodium or no-salt-added, diced tomatoes (undrained)

Directions:

1. Use a cooking spray to coat a big pot. Add and cook beef for 5-7 minutes over medium-high heat, frequently stirring to break up the meat. Drain excess fat in a strainer by rinsing with water.
2. Return the meat to the pot. Cook for 5 minutes, stirring periodically, after adding the chili powder, garlic, bell pepper, and cumin. Bring the remaining ingredients to a boil.
3. Bring the heat to a low, cover, and cook for 20 minutes. If desired, serve with fat-free sour cream, low-fat grated cheese, sliced avocado, chopped green onions, or trimmed cilantro.

Per serving: Calories: 297kcal; Fat: 6g; Carbs: 29g; Protein: 31g; Saturated Fat: 1g; Cholesterol: 62mg; Sugar: 8g

CHAPTER 5: Vegan and Vegetarian

54. Spinach, Walnut, And Black Bean Burgers

Difficulty: ★★★☆☆
Preparation time: 10 minutes
Cooking time: 20 minutes
Servings: 6 Patties
Ingredients:

- 1 tablespoon olive oil
- 1 white onion, diced
- 1 cup spinach and walnut pesto
- 2 (19-ounce) cans of low-sodium black beans, drained and rinsed
- 2 large eggs
- ½ cup whole wheat or whole-grain bread crumbs

Directions:

1. Preheat the oven to 375°F. Line a baking sheet with parchment paper.
2. Heat the olive oil over high heat in a skillet and sauté the onion until translucent, about 3 minutes.
3. Put the onion, Spinach and Walnut Pesto, beans, eggs, and bread crumbs into a blender or food processor and pulse until combined.
4. Using a ½-cup scoop, form 6 patties and place them on the prepared baking sheet.
5. Bake the patties in the oven for 20 minutes. Enjoy immediately.

Per serving: Calories: 383kcal; Fat: 4g; Carbs: 32g; Protein: 12g; Saturated Fat: 1g; Cholesterol: 23mg; Sugar: 1g

55. Artichokes alla Romana

Difficulty: ★★★☆☆
Preparation time: 15 minutes
Cooking time: 50 minutes
Servings: 8

Ingredients:

- 1 tablespoon of olive oil
- 2 cups of fresh whole-wheat breadcrumbs,
- One teaspoon of fresh oregano; chopped.
- Four artichokes; large globe
- 1/3 cup of grated Parmesan cheese
- 2 halved lemons,
- 1 cup of dry white wine
- Three finely chopped garlic cloves,
- 1 tablespoon of grated lemon zest
- Two tablespoons of fresh flat-leaf finely chopped (Italian) parsley.
- 1 cup and 2 to 4 tablespoons of low-sodium chicken stock or vegetable
- One tablespoon of minced shallot
- 1/4 teaspoon of black pepper; freshly ground.

Directions:

1. Set the oven to 400 degrees Fahrenheit. Combine the olive oil and breadcrumbs in a mixing dish. Toss to coat evenly. Place the crumbs in a baking pan and bake it until gently brown for approximately 10 minutes, stirring once halfway through. Allow cooling before serving.
2. Snip off tough outer leaves and cut the stem flush with the base, one artichoke at a time. The top third of the leaves are cut off with a serrated knife, and scissors remove any remaining thorns. To avoid discoloration, rub the sliced edges with half of a lemon. Remove the tiny leaves from the middle and separate the inner leaves. Scoop out the fuzzy choke using a spoon or melon baller, then pour

lemon juice into the hollow. Trim the rest of the artichokes the same way.

3. Stir the breadcrumbs with parsley, Parmesan, lemon zest, garlic, and pepper in a large mixing bowl. Add the 2 to 4 tbsp. of stock, only 1 tbsp. at a time, 'til the stuffing begins to cling together in tiny clumps.

4. Make a small mound in the middle of the artichokes with 2/3 of the filling. Spread the leaves wide, beginning at the bottom, and spoon a rounded spoonful of filling at the base of each leaf. (You may prepare the artichokes up to this stage ahead of time and keep them refrigerated.)

5. Combine shallot, wine, 1 cup stock, and oregano in a Dutch oven with a tight-fitting lid. (Note: If you cook the artichokes in cast iron, they will become brown.) Boil it, then turn off the heat. Arrange the artichokes in one layer in the liquid, stems down. Cover and cook for 45 minutes until the outer leaves are soft (add water if necessary). Place the artichokes on a cooling rack to cool gently. Each artichoke should be quartered and served warm.

Per serving: Calories: 123kcal; Fat: 3g; Carbs: 18g; Protein: 6g; Saturated Fat: 1g; Cholesterol: 3mg; Sugar: 2g

56. Loaded Veggie-Stuffed Peppers

Difficulty: ★★★★☆
Preparation time: 15 minutes
Cooking time: 1 hour
Servings: 6 Peppers
Ingredients:

- ½ cup brown rice, rinsed
- 1 cup water
- 1 (19-ounce) can of low-sodium black beans, drained and rinsed

- 1 (12-ounce) can of low-sodium corn, drained
- 1 cup fresh lime salsa
- Six orange bell peppers halved top to bottom and seeded
- olive oil

Directions:

1. In a medium saucepan over high heat, combine the rice and water and bring to a boil. Cover, reduce the heat to low, then simmer until the liquid is absorbed, about 30 minutes. Remove from the heat, fluff with a fork, and let cool.

2. Preheat the oven to 375°F. Line a baking sheet with parchment paper.

3. Mix the rice, black beans, corn, and Fresh Lime Salsa in a medium bowl.

4. Lightly brush the outside of the bell pepper halves with oil.

5. Evenly distribute the bean mixture among the bell pepper halves. Place the peppers on the prepared baking sheet and cover them with aluminum foil.

6. Bake the stuffed peppers for 20 minutes, remove the foil, and bake for another 10 minutes until fragrant. Enjoy immediately.

Per serving: Calories: 279kcal; Fat: 3g; Carbs: 56g; Protein: 11g; Saturated Fat: 1g; Cholesterol: 0mg; Sugar: 8g

57. Lentils And Pasta

Difficulty: ★★★★☆
Preparation time: 10 minutes
Cooking time: 60 minutes
Servings: 6
Ingredients:

- 1 cup lentils
- 1/2 cup celery, sliced
- 1 1/2 cups onion, coarsely chopped, divided
- 2 tablespoons olive oil

- 1/2 teaspoon cumin
- 1 tablespoon cilantro
- 6 ounces of fresh spinach
- 8 ounces pasta (small shapes like orzo are best)

Directions:

1. Cook lentils in 6 cups (1.4 L) water with celery and 1 1/2 cups (80 g) of the onion until soft, about 40 minutes. Heat the olive oil and sauté the remaining onions, cumin, and cilantro until the onions are soft in a large skillet.
2. Add spinach and sauté until wilted, another 4 to 5 minutes. Drain lentils and stir into the onion-spinach mixture. Cook pasta according to package directions. Stir into mixture.

Per serving: Calories: 245kcal; Fat: 5g; Carbs: 40g; Protein: 10g; Saturated Fat: 1g; Cholesterol: 0mg; Sugar: 5g

58. English Cucumber Salad With Balsamic Vinaigrette

Difficulty: ★★☆☆☆
Preparation time: 15 minutes
Cooking time: 0 minutes
Servings: 4
Ingredients:

- Cracked black pepper, to taste.
- 1 English cucumber washed and thinly sliced, with peel (8 to 9 inches in length),

For the dressing:

- 2 tablespoons of balsamic vinegar
- One tablespoon of fresh rosemary, finely chopped.
- 1 tablespoon of Dijon mustard
- 1 1/2 tablespoons of olive oil

Directions:

1. Combine the vinegar, rosemary, and olive oil in a small saucepan. Heat for 5 minutes over very low heat to combine and enhance the flavors. Remove the pan from the heat and whisk in the mustard until smooth.
2. Place the cucumber slices in a serving dish. Toss the cucumbers in the dressing to coat them evenly. Toss in a pinch of black pepper to taste. Place in the refrigerator until ready to serve.

Per serving: Calories: 67kcal; Fat: 5g; Carbs: 5g; Protein: 1g; Saturated Fat: 2g; Cholesterol: 0mg; Sugar: 3g

59. Mango Black Bean Salsa

Difficulty: ★★☆☆☆
Preparation time: 15 minutes
Cooking time: 0 minutes
Servings: 12
Ingredients:

- One can (15 oz) of black beans, rinsed, then drained
- One medium mango, peeled and cubed
- 1/4 cup finely chopped onion
- 1/4 cup minced fresh cilantro
- tablespoons lime juice
- 1 teaspoon garlic salt
- 1/4 teaspoon ground cumin
- Baked tortilla chip scoops

Directions:

1. In a large bowl, mix all ingredients except chips. Refrigerate until serving. Serve with chips.

Per serving: Calories: 70kcal; Fat: 0g; Carbs: 14g; Protein: 3g; Saturated Fat: 0g; Cholesterol: 0mg; Sugar: 5g

60. Butternut Squash And Apple Salad

Difficulty: ★★★☆☆
Preparation time: 10 minutes
Cooking time: 30 minutes
Servings: 6
Ingredients:

- 2 teaspoons of olive oil

- One peeled and seeded butternut squash, 1/2-inch pieces (8 cups)
- Two large cored and sliced apples, 1/2-inch pieces
- 1 1/2 cups of chopped celery
- 6 cups of chopped spinach,
- 2 cups of chopped carrots
- 6 cups of chopped arugula

Dressing:

- 1 1/2 teaspoons of honey
- 2 teaspoons of balsamic vinegar
- 1/2 cup of plain low-fat yogurt

Directions:

1. Preheat the oven to 400 degrees Fahrenheit. Squash is tossed in olive oil and roasted for 20 to 30 minutes until golden brown and tender.
2. Allow cooling completely. In a large mixing bowl, combine all of the veggies. Whisk together the vinegar, yogurt, and honey to make the dressing. Whisk until the mixture is completely smooth. Dress the salad with the dressing. Toss it and enjoy it.

Per serving: Calories: 215kcal; Fat: 3g; Carbs: 42g; Protein: 5g; Saturated Fat: 1g; Cholesterol: 1mg; Sugar: 6g

61. Yellow Pear And Cherry Tomato Salad

Difficulty: ★★☆☆☆
Preparation time: 25 minutes
Cooking time: 0 minutes
Servings: 6
Ingredients:
For the vinaigrette

- One tablespoon of minced shallot
- 1/4 teaspoon of salt
- 1 tablespoon of extra-virgin olive oil
- 1 1/2 cups of halved yellow pear tomatoes,

- 1/8 teaspoon of black pepper; freshly ground.
- 2 tablespoons of red wine vinegar or sherry vinegar
- 1 1/2 cups of halved orange cherry tomatoes,
- Four fresh large basil leaves smash into slender ribbons.
- 1 1/2 cups of halved red cherry tomatoes

Directions:

1. To prepare the vinaigrette, mix the shallot and vinegar in a small dish and set aside for 15 minutes.
2. Whisk in the salt, olive oil, and pepper until thoroughly combined. Toss the tomatoes together in a large serving bowl or salad bowl.
3. Stir the tomatoes in the vinaigrette, add the basil and toss lightly to coat evenly. Serve immediately.

Per serving: Calories: 47kcal; Fat: 3g; Carbs: 4g; Protein: 1g; Saturated Fat: 1g; Cholesterol: 0mg; Sugar: 4g

62. Ambrosia With Coconut And Toasted Almonds

Difficulty: ★★☆☆☆
Preparation time: 20 minutes
Cooking time: 10 minutes
Servings: 8
Ingredients:

- One small, cubed pineapple (about 3 cups)
- 1/2 cup of shredded coconut; unsweetened
- Two cored and diced red apples
- 5 segmented oranges,
- One peeled banana was halved lengthwise and sliced crosswise.
- 1/2 cup of slivered almonds
- For Garnish: Fresh mint leaves

- 2 tablespoons of cream sherry

Directions:

1. Set the oven to 325 degrees Fahrenheit. Spread the almonds on a baking sheet and bake for 10 minutes, stirring periodically, until brown and fragrant. Immediately transfer to a platter to cool. Place coconut on the sheet and bake, often stirring, until the coconut is lightly toasted, for approximately 10 minutes. Immediately transfer to a platter to cool.

2. Combine the banana, oranges, pineapple, apples, and sherry in a large mixing bowl. Toss lightly to combine. Using separate bowls, divide the fruit mixture equally. The roasted almonds and coconut are uniformly distributed, and the mint is used as a garnish. Serve right away.

Per serving: Calories: 177kcal; Fat: 5g; Carbs: 30g; Protein: 3g; Saturated Fat: 1g; Cholesterol: 0mg; Sugar: 3g

63. Broccoli Wild Rice Casserole

Difficulty: ★★★☆☆
Preparation time: 10 minutes
Cooking time: 60 minutes
Servings: 6
Ingredients:

- 1 1/2 cups wild rice
- 6 cups broccoli
- 2 cups reduced-sodium cream of mushroom soup
- 2 cups low-fat cheddar cheese, shredded

Directions:

1. Preheat the oven to 325 deg. F (gas mark 3) before starting. Prepare wild rice as directed on the package.

2. Layer rice in the bottom of a 9 × 9-inch (23 x 23-cm) casserole pan. Broccoli should be steamed for 5 minutes before being layered on top of rice.

3. Toss the soup with the cheese and distribute it on top of the broccoli. Bake for 45 minutes, uncovered.

Per serving: Calories: 293kcal; Fat: 5g; Carbs: 44g; Protein: 20g; Saturated Fat: 1g; Cholesterol: 12mg; Sugar: 6g

64. Chipotle Lime Avocado Salad

Difficulty: ★★☆☆☆
Preparation time: 15 minutes
Cooking time: 0 minutes
Servings: 4
Ingredients:

- 1/4 cup lime juice
- 1/4 cup of maple syrup
- 1/2 teaspoon chipotle pepper, ground
- 1/4 teaspoon cayenne pepper
- Two peeled and sliced medium ripe avocados
- peeled and sliced 1/2 a medium cucumber
- a tablespoon of fresh chives, minced
- large tomatoes, peeled and cut into 1/2-inch thick slices

Directions:

1. Whisk lime juice, maple syrup, chipotle pepper, and, if preferred, cayenne pepper together in a small bowl until well combined.

2. Combine avocados, cucumber, and chives in a separate bowl. Drizzle dressing over the salad and gently mix to coat. Serve with tomatoes on the side.

Per serving: Calories: 191kcal; Fat: 11g; Carbs: 25g; Protein: 3g; Saturated Fat: 2g; Cholesterol: 0mg; Sugar: 7g

65. Grilled Vegetable Orzo Salad

Difficulty: ★★★☆☆
Preparation time: 10 minutes
Cooking time: 20 minutes
Servings: 8

Ingredients:

- 1 cup zucchini, cut into 1" (2.5-cm) cubes
- 1 cup red onion, cut into 1" (2.5-cm) cubes
- 1/2 teaspoon minced garlic
- Three tablespoons of olive oil, divided
- 1/2 cup yellow bell pepper, cut into 1" (2.5-cm) cubes
- One teaspoon of freshly ground black pepper, divided
- 1/2 cup red bell pepper, cut into 1" (2.5-cm) cubes
- 8-ounce orzo
- 1/3 cup lemon juice
- 1/4 cup pine nuts, toasted

Directions:

1. Prepare the grill. Toss zucchini, bell peppers, onion, and garlic in a large bowl with one tablespoon olive oil and 1/2 teaspoon pepper. Transfer to a grill basket. Grill for 15 to 20 minutes, or 'til browned, stirring occasionally. Meanwhile, cook the orzo according to the package directions. Drain and transfer to a large serving bowl.
2. Add the roasted vegetables to the pasta. Combine the lemon juice, remaining olive oil, and pepper and pour on the pasta and vegetables. Let cool to room temperature. Stir in the pine nuts.

Per serving: Calories: 201kcal; Fat: 9g; Carbs: 27g; Protein: 5g; Saturated Fat: 3g; Cholesterol: 0mg; Sugar: 6g

CHAPTER 6: Soups And Stews

66. Gluten-Free Asparagus Soup

Difficulty: ★★★☆☆
Preparation time: 10 minutes
Cooking time: 20 minutes
Servings: 4
Ingredients:

- 1 ½ lbs asparagus, trimmed & chopped
- 4 cups vegetable broth
- 14 oz can white beans, drained & rinsed
- 1 tbsp sesame oil
- 1 tsp garlic, chopped
- 1 onion, chopped
- Pepper
- Salt

Directions:

1. Heat oil into the pot over medium heat.
2. Add onion and sauté for 4 minutes. Add garlic and sauté for a minute.
3. Add remaining ingredients and stir well. Bring to boil.
4. Turn the heat to low and simmer for 10 minutes. Remove pot from heat.
5. Puree the soup using a blender until smooth.
6. Stir well and serve.

Per serving: Calories: 172kcal; Fat: 5g; Carbs: 25g; Protein: 10g; Saturated Fat: 1g; Cholesterol: 0mg; Sugar: 4g

67. Gazpacho

Difficulty: ★★☆☆☆
Preparation time: 20 minutes
Cooking time: 0 minutes
Servings: 4
Ingredients:

- Four large beefsteak tomatoes, chopped
- 1 cup yellow or red cherry tomatoes, chopped
- 1 cup grape tomatoes, chopped
- One cucumber, peeled, seeded, and chopped
- 3 scallions, sliced
- 1 clove of garlic, minced
- 1 cup low-sodium tomato juice
- 1 tablespoon fresh lemon juice
- 1 tablespoon olive oil
- Pinch salt
- ⅛ teaspoon white pepper
- dash tabasco sauce
- 2 tablespoons chopped fresh dill

Directions:

1. In a large bowl, combine the beefsteak tomatoes, cherry tomatoes, grape tomatoes, cucumber, scallions, garlic, tomato juice, lemon juice, olive oil, salt, white pepper, Tabasco, and fresh dill.
2. Use an immersion blender to blend about half of the soup. You can also mash some of the ingredients with a potato masher. Or put about ⅓ of the soup mixture into a blender or food processor. Blend or process until smooth then returns the blended mixture to the rest of the soup.
3. Serve immediately, or cover and chill for a few hours.

Per serving: Calories: 115kcal; Fat: 4g; Carbs: 19g; Protein: 4g; Saturated Fat: 1g; Cholesterol: 0mg; Sugar: 2g

68. Flavors Corn Soup

Difficulty: ★★★★☆
Preparation time: 10 minutes
Cooking time: 8 hours
Servings: 8
Ingredients:

- 20 oz can corn, drained

- 3 cups vegetable broth
- 1/2 tsp coriander powder
- ½ tsp thyme
- 1 tsp cumin powder
- 1 ½ jalapeno pepper, seeded & chopped
- 2 large potatoes, cut into chunks
- Pepper
- Salt

Directions:

1. Add corn and remaining ingredients into the slow cooker and stir everything well.
2. Cover and cook on low for 8 hours.
3. Stir well and serve.

Per serving: Calories: 125kcal; Fat: 1g; Carbs: 28g; Protein: 4g; Saturated Fat: 0g; Cholesterol: 0mg; Sugar: 5g

69. Easy Pea Soup

Difficulty: ★★★☆☆
Preparation time: 10 minutes
Cooking time: 20 minutes
Servings: 6
Ingredients:

- 2 cups split peas
- 8 cups vegetable broth
- 1 tsp dried oregano
- 1 tbsp garlic, chopped
- 2 carrots, chopped
- 2 celery stalks, chopped
- 1 tbsp sesame oil
- 1 onion, chopped
- Pepper
- Salt

Directions:

1. Add oil into the instant pot, then set the pot on sauté mode.
2. Add carrots, celery, onion, and sauté for 5 minutes—season with pepper and salt. Turn off sauté mode.
3. Add remaining ingredients and stir well.

4. Cover and cook on high for 15 minutes.
5. Once cooking is done, then allow releasing pressure naturally. Remove lid.
6. Puree the soup using a blender 'til smooth.
7. Serve and enjoy.

Per serving: Calories: 314kcal; Fat: 5g; Carbs: 45g; Protein: 23g; Saturated Fat: 1g; Cholesterol: 0mg; Sugar: 1g

70. Potato Squash Soup

Difficulty: ★★★☆☆
Preparation time: 10 minutes
Cooking time: 22 minutes
Servings: 4
Ingredients:

- 2 large summer squash, cut into half
- 2 tbsp fresh lemon juice
- ½ cup unsweetened coconut milk
- 4 cups vegetable broth
- 1 tbsp olive oil
- 1 tsp garlic, minced
- 1 potato, peeled & diced
- 1 yellow onion, diced
- Pepper
- Salt

Directions:

1. Heat oil into the pot over medium heat.
2. Add all veggies and sauté for 5 minutes.
3. Add broth and stir well, and bring to boil.
4. Turn heat to low and simmer vegetables for 15-20 minutes. Remove from heat.
5. Puree the soup using a blender until smooth.
6. Stir in lemon juice and coconut milk. Season with pepper and salt.
7. Serve and enjoy.

Per serving: Calories: 200kcal; Fat: 12g; Carbs: 17g; Protein: 8g; Saturated Fat: 4g; Cholesterol: 0mg; Sugar: 9g

71. Healthy Mushroom Soup

Difficulty: ★★☆☆☆
Preparation time: 10 minutes
Cooking time: 5 minutes
Servings: 1
Ingredients:

- ¼ cup mushrooms, chopped
- ½ cup unsweetened almond milk
- ¾ cup vegetable broth
- 2 tbsp olive oil
- 3 tbsp rice flour
- Pepper
- Salt

Directions:

1. Heat oil into the saucepan over medium heat.
2. Add mushrooms and sauté until softened.
3. Add flour and cook for a minute. Add broth and milk and stir well.
4. Turn heat to low and simmer until thickened. Season with pepper and salt.
5. Stir well and serve.

Per serving: Calories: 377kcal; Fat: 30g; Carbs: 26g; Protein: 3g; Saturated Fat: 5g; Cholesterol: 0mg; Sugar: 8g

72. Flavors Vegetable Stew

Difficulty: ★★★★☆
Preparation time: 10 minutes
Cooking time: 8 hours
Servings: 6
Ingredients:

- 1 cup frozen peas
- 1 cup frozen corn
- 2 lbs potatoes, peeled & cubed
- 4 large carrots, peeled & diced
- 1 medium onion, chopped
- ½ cup unsweetened coconut milk
- ½ tsp dried oregano
- 1 tsp garlic powder
- 4 cups vegetable broth
- Pepper
- Salt

Directions:

1. Add all ingredients except coconut milk into the slow cooker and stir well.
2. Cover and cook on low for 8 hours.
3. Stir in coconut milk and serve.

Per serving: Calories: 226kcal; Fat: 5g; Carbs: 41g; Protein: 6g; Saturated Fat: 2g; Cholesterol: 0mg; Sugar: 4g

73. Lentil Veggie Stew

Difficulty: ★★★★☆
Preparation time: 10 minutes
Cooking time: 4 hours
Servings: 8
Ingredients:

- 1 cup green lentils, rinsed
- ¼ cup olive oil
- ¼ tsp chili powder
- ½ tsp dried thyme
- ½ tsp dried oregano
- ½ cup wheat berries
- 4 cups vegetable broth
- 1 tsp garlic, minced
- 2 potatoes, peeled & diced
- 3 carrots, peeled & diced
- 2 celery stalks, sliced
- 1 medium onion, chopped
- Pepper
- Salt

Directions:

1. Add green lentils and remaining ingredients into the slow cooker and stir well.
2. Cover and cook on high for 4 hours.
3. Stir well and serve.

Per serving: Calories: 209kcal; Fat: 7g; Carbs: 30g; Protein: 8g; Saturated Fat: 3g; Cholesterol: 0mg; Sugar: 4g

74. Silky Zucchini Soup

Difficulty: ★★★☆☆
Preparation time: 10 minutes
Cooking time: 30 minutes
Servings: 4
Ingredients:

- 6 cups zucchini, chopped
- 1 ½ cups vegetable broth
- 1 tbsp olive oil
- 1 tbsp garlic, minced
- 1 medium onion, chopped
- ¼ tsp chili powder
- Pepper
- Salt

Directions:

1. Heat oil into the pot over medium heat.
2. Add onion and sauté for 5 minutes.
3. Add garlic and sauté for a minute.
4. Add zucchini, chili powder, pepper, and salt, and sauté for 10 minutes.
5. Add broth and stir well, reduce heat and simmer for 15 minutes.
6. Puree the soup using a blender until smooth.
7. Serve and enjoy.

Per serving: Calories: 74kcal; Fat: 4g; Carbs: 9g; Protein: 3g; Saturated Fat: 1g; Cholesterol: 0mg; Sugar: 4g

75. Chickpea Sweet Potato Stew

Difficulty: ★★★★☆
Preparation time: 10 minutes
Cooking time: 4 hours 5 minutes
Servings: 4
Ingredients:

- 2 medium sweet potatoes, chopped
- 14 oz can chickpeas, drained & rinsed
- 1/8 tsp cayenne
- ½ tsp turmeric
- ½ tsp cinnamon
- 1 tsp smoked paprika
- 1 ½ tsp garam masala
- 1 tsp ground coriander
- 1 cup vegetable broth
- 2 cups canned tomatoes, crushed
- 1 tbsp garlic, chopped
- 1 tbsp olive oil
- 1 onion, chopped
- Pepper
- Salt

Directions:

1. Preheat the oil in a pan over medium-high heat.
2. Add onion and then sauté for 3 minutes.
3. Add garlic and sauté for a minute.
4. Transfer sautéed onion and remaining ingredients into the slow cooker and stir well.
5. Cover and cook on high for 4 hours.
6. Stir well and serve.

Per serving: Calories: 283kcal; Fat: 5g; Carbs: 54g; Protein: 8g; Saturated Fat: 2g; Cholesterol: 0mg; Sugar: 5g

CHAPTER 7: Snacks And Sides

76. Old Bay Crispy Kale Chips

Difficulty: ★★★☆☆
Preparation time: 10 minutes
Cooking time: 25 minutes
Servings: 4
Ingredients:

- bunch kale washed
- tablespoons olive oil
- 1 to 3 teaspoons Old Bay Seasoning
- Sea salt, to taste

Directions:

1. Preheat the oven to 300 °F. Remove the kale's tough stems and shred the leaves into large pieces. Combine all of the ingredients in a large mixing bowl. Toss with olive oil and spices to coat. Arrange the leaves on prepared baking sheets in a single layer.
2. Bake for 10 minutes, uncovered, before rotating pans. Bake for 15 minutes, or 'til crisp and beginning to brown. Allow at least 5 minutes to stand before serving.

Per serving: Calories: 101kcal; Fat: 7g; Carbs: 8g; Protein: 3g; Saturated Fat: 2g; Cholesterol: 0mg; Sugar: 2g

77. Nutty Broccoli Slaw

Difficulty: ★★☆☆☆
Preparation time: 15 minutes
Cooking time: 0 minutes
Servings: 16
Ingredients:

- 2 cups of sliced green onions: 2 bunches
- package of chicken ramen noodles (3 ounces)
- 1-1/2 cups of broccoli florets
- One package of broccoli coleslaw mix; (16 ounces)
- One can of ripe olives (6 ounces); drained and halved
- 1 cup of sunflower kernels, toasted
- 1/2 cup of slivered almonds, toasted
- 1/2 cup cider vinegar
- 1/2 cup of sugar
- 1/2 cup olive oil

Directions:

1. Open the noodle seasoning package and put the crushed noodles in a large mixing bowl. Combine the onions, sunflower kernels, broccoli, slaw mix, olives, and almonds.
2. Combine the seasoning package's oil, vinegar, sugar, and contents in a jar with a tight-fitting cover; shake thoroughly. Drizzle the dressing over the salad and toss to combine. Serve right away.

Per serving: Calories: 206kcal; Fat: 15g; Carbs: 16g; Protein: 4g; Saturated Fat: 5g; Cholesterol: 0mg; Sugar: 2g

78. Hummus

Difficulty: ★★☆☆☆
Preparation time: 25 minutes
Cooking time: 20 minutes plus chilling
Servings: 1 1/2 cup
Ingredients:

- 1/4 cup of fresh lemon juice
- 1/2 teaspoon of baking soda
- 1/2 teaspoon of kosher salt
- can (15 ounces) garbanzo beans/chickpeas: rinsed & drained
- 1 tablespoon of minced garlic
- 1/2 cup of tahini
- 1/2 teaspoon of ground cumin
- tablespoons of extra virgin olive oil

- Optional: roasted garbanzo beans, Olive oil, ground sumac, toasted sesame seeds,
- 1/4 cup of cold water

Directions:

1. Place the garbanzo beans and enough water to cover them by 1 inch in a large saucepan. Rub the beans together gently to release the outer skin. Pour off the water as well as any floating skins. Drain 2-3 times after repeating steps unless no skins float to the top. Return to saucepan; stir in baking soda and 1 inch of water. Bring to a boil, then turn off the heat. Cook for 20-25 minutes until beans are soft and begin to come apart.
2. Meanwhile, puree the garlic, lemon juice, and salt in a blender until smooth. Allow 10 minutes to stand before straining and discarding the solids. Cumin is added at this point. Combine tahini and olive oil in a small bowl.
3. Blend the beans with the cold water in a blender. Cover loosely with cover and process until absolutely smooth. Stir in the lemon mixture in the food processor. Slowly drizzle in the tahini mixture while the blender runs, scraping down the sides as required. If desired, add more salt and cumin to the seasoning. Refrigerate for at least 30 minutes after transferring the mixture to the serving bowl. Additional toppings or olive oil may be added if desired.

Per serving: Calories: 250kcal; Fat: 19g; Carbs: 15g; Protein: 7g; Saturated Fat: 5g; Cholesterol: 0mg; Sugar: 4g

79. Pita Chips

Difficulty: ★★☆☆☆
Preparation time: 10 minutes
Cooking time: 10 minutes
Servings: 4
Ingredients:

- 1/4 tsp of garlic powder
- 1 Tbsp. of grated Parmesan cheese
- 1/2 tsp of salt
- Cooking spray
- 1 Tbsp. of dried Italian seasoning
- (6-inch) pita bread (whole wheat)

Directions:

1. Preheat the oven to 350 degrees Fahrenheit. Combine Parmesan, garlic powder, Italian seasoning, and salt in a mixing bowl. Each pita should be cut into eight wedges and separated into two pieces.
2. Bring on a baking sheet lined with parchment paper, and I used a frying spray to coat the wedges. Season with the seasoning mix and bake for 10 minutes or golden brown. Allow cooling on the rack.

Per serving: Calories: 120kcal; Fat: 3g; Carbs: 20g; Protein: 4g; Saturated Fat: 0g; Cholesterol: 2mg; Sugar: 7g

80. Greek Pizza

Difficulty: ★★★☆☆
Preparation time: 15 minutes
Cooking time: 25 minutes
Servings: 4
Ingredients:

- 1½ cups whole wheat or whole-grain self-rising flour, plus more for dusting
- 1 cup low-fat plain Greek yogurt
- 1½ cups spinach and walnut pesto
- 1 tomato, thinly sliced
- ½ cup thinly sliced white mushrooms

Directions:

1. Preheat the oven to 350°F. Line a baking sheet with parchment paper.
2. In a medium bowl, place the flour. Mix in the yogurt ¼ cup until the dough is smooth. Knead it into a ball.

3. Sprinkle 1 or 2 tablespoons of flour onto a cutting board or hard, clean surface, and form the dough ball into a 12-inch circle.

4. Transfer the dough to the baking sheet and spread it evenly with the Spinach and Walnut Pesto.

5. Arrange the tomato and mushrooms on top of the sauce.

6. Bake the pizza for 25 minutes, 'til the crust is golden brown. Enjoy immediately.

Per serving: Calories: 433kcal; Fat: 31g; Carbs: 33g; Protein: 10g; Saturated Fat: 6g; Cholesterol: 21mg; Sugar: 5g

81. Spicy Almonds

Difficulty: ★★☆☆☆
Preparation time: 10 minutes
Cooking time: 20 minutes
Servings: 6
Ingredients:

- 1 ½ cups almonds
- ½ tsp cayenne
- ¼ tsp onion powder
- ½ tsp garlic powder
- ½ tsp cumin powder
- 1 tsp paprika
- 1 ½ tsp Worcestershire sauce
- Salt

Directions:

1. Preheat the oven to 350 deg. F.

2. In a mixing bowl, mix almonds, Worcestershire sauce, paprika, cumin powder, garlic powder, onion powder, cayenne, and salt until well coated.

3. Spread almonds onto a parchment-lined baking sheet and bake in preheated oven for 15-20 minutes.

4. Serve and enjoy.

Per serving: Calories: 142kcal; Fat: 12g; Carbs: 6g; Protein: 5g; Saturated Fat: 3g; Cholesterol: 0mg; Sugar: 6g

82. Cannellini Bean Hummus

Difficulty: ★★☆☆☆
Preparation time: 10 minutes
Cooking time: 5 minutes
Servings: 16
Ingredients:

- 30 oz can cannellini beans, drained & rinsed
- ¼ cup olive oil
- 1/8 tsp chili powder
- 1 tsp garlic powder
- 1 tsp cumin powder
- 3 tbsp fresh lemon juice
- ¼ cup water
- Salt

Directions:

1. Add beans and remaining ingredients into the food processor and process until desired consistency.

2. Serve and enjoy.

Per serving: Calories: 68kcal; Fat: 3g; Carbs: 9g; Protein: 3g; Saturated Fat: 0g; Cholesterol: 0mg; Sugar: 4g

83. Honey-Lime Berry Salad

Difficulty: ★★☆☆☆
Preparation time: 15 minutes
Cooking time: 0 minutes
Servings: 10
Ingredients:

- 4 cups fresh strawberries, halved
- cups fresh blueberries
- medium Granny Smith apples, cubed
- 1/3 cup lime juice
- 1/4 to 1/3 cup honey
- 2 tablespoons minced fresh mint

Directions:

1. Combine strawberries, blueberries, and apples in a large mixing dish. Combine the lime juice, honey, and mint in a

small mixing bowl. Toss the fruit in the dressing to coat.

Per serving: Calories: 93kcal; Fat: 0g; Carbs: 24g; Protein: 1g; Saturated Fat: 0g; Cholesterol: 0mg; Sugar: 8g

84. Black Bean Dip

Difficulty: ★☆☆☆☆☆
Preparation time: 10 minutes
Cooking time: 5 minutes
Servings: 6
Ingredients:

- 14 oz can black beans, drained & rinsed
- ½ tsp cumin powder
- ¼ cup fresh lemon juice
- ¼ cup sesame oil
- ¼ cup tahini
- 4 garlic cloves
- Salt

Directions:

1. Add black beans and remaining ingredients into the blender and blend until desired consistency.
2. Serve and enjoy.

Per serving: Calories: 197kcal; Fat: 14g; Carbs: 15g; Protein: 5g; Saturated Fat: 3g; Cholesterol: 0mg; Sugar: 6g

85. Crispy Carrot Fries

Difficulty: ★★☆☆☆
Preparation time: 10 minutes
Cooking time: 20 minutes
Servings: 4
Ingredients:

- 3 large carrots, peel & cut into fries shape
- ½ tsp paprika
- ½ tsp onion powder
- 2 tbsp olive oil
- ¼ tsp chili powder
- 1 tsp garlic powder

- Pepper
- Salt

Directions:

1. Preheat your air fryer to 350 deg. F.
2. Tossing carrot fries with remaining ingredients in a mixing bowl until well coated.
3. Add carrot fries into the air fryer basket and cook for 15-20 minutes. Stir halfway through.
4. Serve and enjoy.

Per serving: Calories: 87kcal; Fat: 7g; Carbs: 6g; Protein: 1g; Saturated Fat: 2g; Cholesterol: 0mg; Sugar: 4g

86. Curried Cannellini Bean Dip

Difficulty: ★★☆☆☆
Preparation time: 10 minutes
Cooking time: 5 minutes
Servings: 4
Ingredients:

- 14 oz can cannellini beans, drained & rinsed
- 1 tbsp fresh lemon juice
- 3 tbsp water
- ½ tsp curry powder
- 2 garlic cloves
- 2 tbsp Sriracha sauce
- 1 ½ tsp tamari sauce
- 2 tbsp olive oil
- Salt

Directions:

1. Add cannellini beans and remaining ingredients into the blender and blend until smooth and creamy.
2. Serve and enjoy.

Per serving: Calories: 396kcal; Fat: 8g; Carbs: 60g; Protein: 24g; Saturated Fat: 2g; Cholesterol: 0mg; Sugar: 5g

87. Winter Perfect Guacamole

Difficulty: ★☆☆☆☆
Preparation time: 10 minutes
Cooking time: 5 minutes
Servings: 8
Ingredients:

- 3 avocados, peel, pitted & chopped
- 1 jalapeno pepper, seeded & minced
- 1 tsp garlic, chopped
- ½ tsp cumin
- 1 ½ tbsp fresh lemon juice
- 2 tbsp fresh parsley, chopped
- 1 large pear, core & chopped
- Pepper
- Salt

Directions:

1. In a mixing bowl, mix chopped avocado and the remaining ingredients.
2. Serve and enjoy.

Per serving: Calories: 166kcal; Fat: 15g; Carbs: 9g; Protein: 2g; Saturated Fat: 3g; Cholesterol: 0mg; Sugar: 4g

88. Healthy Beet Dip

Difficulty: ★☆☆☆☆
Preparation time: 10 minutes
Cooking time: 5 minutes
Servings: 6
Ingredients:

- 2 large beets, roasted, peeled& chopped
- ½ cup sesame oil
- ¼ cup fresh lemon juice
- 1 ½ tbsp tahini
- 2 garlic cloves
- 2 tbsp almond flour
- 1 tsp cumin powder
- 1 ¼ cups walnuts
- Salt

Directions:

1. Add chopped beets and remaining ingredients into the blender and blend until desired consistency.
2. Serve and enjoy.

Per serving: Calories: 357kcal; Fat: 35g; Carbs: 7g; Protein: 8g; Saturated Fat: 6g; Cholesterol: 0mg; Sugar: 7g

89. Easy Lentil Dip

Difficulty: ★☆☆☆☆
Preparation time: 10 minutes
Cooking time: 5 minutes
Servings: 4
Ingredients:

- 1 cup cooked lentils
- 1 tsp onion powder
- 2 tbsp vegetable broth
- 2 tbsp peanut butter
- 3 garlic cloves
- 2 tbsp lemon basil vinegar
- 4 tbsp walnuts

Directions:

1. Add cooked lentils and remaining ingredients into the blender and blend until desired consistency.
2. Serve and enjoy.

Per serving: Calories: 285kcal; Fat: 10g; Carbs: 34g; Protein: 17g; Saturated Fat: 2g; Cholesterol: 0mg; Sugar: 2g

CHAPTER 8: Salads

90. Beet Walnut Salad

Difficulty: ★★☆☆☆
Preparation time: 20 minutes
Cooking time: 0 minutes
Servings: 8
Ingredients:

- 1/4 cup of red wine vinegar
- One small bunch of beets, or canned beets (no salt added) for 3 cups, drained.
- 3 tablespoons of balsamic vinegar
- 1/4 cup of chopped celery
- 1 tablespoon of olive oil
- 1/4 cup of crumbled gorgonzola cheese
- 8 cups of fresh salad greens
- 1 tablespoon of water
- Three tablespoons of chopped walnuts
- 1/4 cup of chopped apple
- Freshly ground pepper.

Directions:

1. In a saucepan, steam raw beets in water in the saucepan until soft. Skins should be slipped off. Cool by rinsing. Using a cutter, slice it into 1/2-inch rounds. Toss with red wine vinegar in a medium mixing bowl.
2. Combine the olive oil, balsamic vinegar, and water in a large mixing bowl. Toss in the salad greens.
3. Arrange salad greens on separate salad plates. Add apples, sliced beets, and celery to the top. Pepper, cheese, and walnuts are placed over the top. Serve immediately.

Per serving: Calories: 105kcal; Fat: 5g; Carbs: 12g; Protein: 3g; Saturated Fat: 1g; Cholesterol: 5mg; Sugar: 5g

91. French Green Lentil Salad

Difficulty: ★★★☆☆
Preparation time: 10 minutes
Cooking time: 30 minutes
Servings: 6
Ingredients:

- 1/2 yellow finely chopped onion,
- Four tablespoons of olive oil, divided.
- 3 minced cloves of garlic,
- 4-inch-piece of finely chopped celery stalk,
- One teaspoon of mustard seed
- 4-inch-piece of peeled and finely chopped carrot,
- 1 teaspoon of fennel seed
- 1/2 cup of water
- 2 cups of chicken stock or broth, vegetable stock,
- 1 bay leaf
- One cup of French green lentils; rinsed, picked over, then drained.
- 1/4 teaspoon of black pepper; freshly ground.
- 1 tablespoon of Dijon mustard
- One tablespoon of fresh chopped thyme /1 teaspoon of dried thyme
- 2 tablespoons of flat-leaf fresh (Italian) parsley, slice into strips
- 1 tablespoon of sherry vinegar or red wine vinegar

Directions:

1. Two teaspoons of olive oil are heated in a large saucepan over medium heat. Add and sauté the celery, onion, and carrot for approximately 5 minutes or soften the veggies. Add and sauté the mustard

seed, garlic, and fennel seed for 1 minute, or until the spices are aromatic.

2. Add the water, stock, thyme, lentils, and bay leaf. Boil the water over medium-high heat. Bring the heat to low, partly cover, and cook for 25 to 30 minutes until the lentils are cooked but firm. Drain the lentils and keep the cooking liquid aside. Remove the bay leaf and transfer the lentils to a large mixing bowl.

3. Combine the mustard, vinegar, and 1/4 cup of the leftover cooking liquid in a small dish. (Any leftover liquid should be discarded or saved for subsequent use.) In a separate bowl, whisk together the remaining olive oil. Toss the lentils lightly with the parsley, vinaigrette, and pepper to coat evenly. Warm the dish before serving.

Per serving: Calories: 189kcal; Fat: 5g; Carbs: 25g; Protein: 11g; Saturated Fat: 2g; Cholesterol: 2mg; Sugar: 4g

92. Braised Celery Root

Difficulty: ★★★☆☆
Preparation time: 10 minutes
Cooking time: 10 minutes
Servings: 6
Ingredients:

- 1 cup of vegetable broth or stock
- One peeled and diced celery root (celeriac) (about 3 cups)
- 1/4 cup of sour cream
- 1 teaspoon of Dijon mustard
- 1/4 teaspoon of salt
- 1/4 teaspoon of black pepper; freshly ground.
- 2 teaspoons of fresh thyme leaves

Directions:

1. Boil the stock in a large saucepan over high heat. Add the celery root and mix well. Reduce the heat to low when the

stock resumes to a boil. Cover and cook, occasionally turning, for 10 to 12 minutes, or until the soft celery root.

2. Shift the celery root to a bowl with a slotted spoon, cover, and keep warm. Raise the heat to high and boil the cooking liquid in the saucepan. Cook, uncovered, for 5 minutes or 'til the liquid has been reduced to 1 tablespoon.

3. Whisk in the mustard, salt, sour cream, and pepper after removing the pan from the heat. Stir in the thyme and celery root until the sauce is well cooked over medium heat. Immediately transfer to a hot serving dish and serve.

Per serving: Calories: 54kcal; Fat: 2g; Carbs: 7g; Protein: 2g; Saturated Fat: 1g; Cholesterol: 4mg; Sugar: 4g

93. Waldorf Salad With Yogurt

Difficulty: ★★☆☆☆
Preparation time: 20 minutes
Cooking time: 0 minutes
Servings: 4
Ingredients:

- One tablespoon of lemon juice
- Three cored peeled and chopped tart apples.
- 1 cup of seedless grapes
- 2 tablespoons of chopped walnuts
- Two chopped stalks of celery,
- ¼ teaspoon of celery seed
- 2 chopped green onions,
- 3 tablespoons of apple juice
- 2 tablespoons of mayonnaise
- One bunch of trimmed and chopped watercress
- 2 tablespoons of plain yogurt

Directions:

1. Combine the lemon juice and apples in a large mixing bowl. Toss with celery, grapes, and green onions.

2. Whisk the yogurt, apple juice, grapes, and celery seeds in a small bowl. Pour over the apple mixture and gently stir. Wash and dry the watercress completely. Top with a mound of apple mixture and a sprinkling of walnuts. Arrange the greens on separate salad plates.

Per serving: Calories: 180kcal; Fat: 9g; Carbs: 26g; Protein: 3g; Saturated Fat: 2g; Cholesterol: 4mg; Sugar: 1g

94. Spinach Berry Salad

Difficulty: ★☆☆☆☆
Preparation time: 10 minutes
Cooking time: 0 minutes
Servings: 4
Ingredients:

- 1 cup of fresh sliced strawberries
- Four packed cups of torn fresh spinach
- 1 cup frozen or fresh blueberries
- 1/4 cup of pecan: chopped, toasted.
- One small sliced sweet onion,

Salad dressing:

- 1/8 teaspoon of pepper
- 2 tablespoons of balsamic vinegar
- 2 tablespoons of honey
- One teaspoon of curry powder (can be omitted)
- 2 teaspoons of Dijon mustard
- 2 tablespoons of white wine vinegar or cider vinegar

Directions:

1. Toss onion, spinach, blueberries, strawberries, and pecans in a large salad bowl. Mix dressing ingredients in a jar with a tight-fitting cover.
2. Shake it vigorously. Mix the salad in the dressing to coat it. Serve immediately.

Per serving: Calories: 158kcal; Fat: 5g; Carbs: 25g; Protein: 4g; Saturated Fat: 2g; Cholesterol: 0mg; Sugar: 1g

95. Mexican Bean Salad

Difficulty: ★☆☆☆☆
Preparation time: 10 minutes
Cooking time: 0 minutes
Servings: 8
Ingredients:

- 2 cups cooked kidney beans
- 2 cups cooked garbanzo beans
- 1 cup tomatoes, chopped
- 3/4 cup cucumber, peeled & chopped
- 4 cups lettuce, shredded
- 1/2 cup avocado, mashed
- 2 tablespoons onion, diced
- 1/2 cup plain fat-free yogurt
- 1/4 teaspoon minced garlic
- 1/2 teaspoon cumin

Directions:

1. Toss the kidney beans, garbanzo beans, tomatoes, cucumber, and onion in a large bowl. Mix the avocado, yogurt, garlic, and cumin in a small bowl.
2. Stir the avocado mixture into the bean mixture and chill. Serve on top of shredded lettuce.

Per serving: Calories: 172kcal; Fat: 3g; Carbs: 29g; Protein: 9g; Saturated Fat: 1g; Cholesterol: 0mg; Sugar: 3g

96. Lemony Kale Salad

Difficulty: ★★☆☆☆
Preparation time: 10 minutes
Cooking time: 10 minutes
Servings: 4
Ingredients:

- 2 heads kale
- Sea salt and freshly ground pepper
- Juice of 1 lemon
- 1 tbsp. olive oil
- 2 cloves garlic, minced
- 1 cup cherry tomatoes, sliced

Directions:

1. Wash and dry kale. Tear the kale into small pieces. Heat olive oil in a huge skillet, then adds the garlic. Cook for 1 minute, and then add the kale.
2. Add the tomatoes after the kale is wilted. Cook until tomatoes are softened, then remove from heat. Add tomatoes and kale to a bowl, and season with sea salt and freshly ground pepper. Sprinkle with remaining olive oil & lemon juice, and serve.

Per serving: Calories: 59kcal; Fat: 4g; Carbs: 6g; Protein: 2g; Saturated Fat: 0g; Cholesterol: 0mg; Sugar: 2g

97. Potato Salad

Difficulty: ★☆☆☆☆
Preparation time: 10 minutes
Cooking time: 0 minutes
Servings: 8
Ingredients:

- 2 tablespoons of minced fresh dill (or 1/2 tablespoon dried)
- 1-pound potatoes, boiled and diced or steamed
- Two ribs celery, diced (1/2 cup)
- One large chopped yellow onion (1 cup)
- 1/4 cup of low-calorie mayonnaise
- One large, diced carrot (1/2 cup)
- One teaspoon of ground black pepper
- 2 tablespoons of red wine vinegar
- 1 tablespoon of Dijon mustard

Directions:

1. In a mixing bowl, mix all ingredients and thoroughly mix them. Before serving, chill it.

Per serving: Calories: 77kcal; Fat: 1g; Carbs: 2g; Protein: 1g; Saturated Fat: 0g; Cholesterol: 2mg; Sugar: 2g

98. Broccoli Salad

Difficulty: ★★★☆☆
Preparation time: 45 minutes
Cooking time: 0 minutes
Servings: 6 cups
Ingredients:

- ¼ cup of red onion; chopped.
- Six cups of fresh broccoli; chopped.
- ½ cup of pumpkin seeds
- ¾ cup of dried cranberries
- ½ cup of mayonnaise
- 2 tablespoons of flax seeds
- 2 tablespoons of raspberry vinegar
- ½ cup of chopped pecans
- 2 tablespoons of white sugar

Directions:

1. Toss the pumpkin seeds, broccoli, cranberries, onion, and flax seeds in a large mixing bowl.
2. Add the vinegar, mayonnaise, and white sugar to a mixing bowl; pour over the salad. Toss to coat evenly. Allow 30 minutes for chilling before serving, then top with pecans

Per serving: Calories: 380kcal; Fat: 28g; Carbs: 29g; Protein: 7g; Saturated Fat: 8g; Cholesterol: 7mg; Sugar: 5g

99. Italian Eggplant Salad

Difficulty: ★★★☆☆
Preparation time: 2 hours 10 minutes
Cooking time: 1 ½ hour
Servings: 12
Ingredients:

- One crushed clove of garlic,
- 6 eggplants
- 1 tablespoon of balsamic vinegar
- ¼ teaspoon of dried basil
- 3 tablespoons of olive oil
- One teaspoon of dried parsley

- 2 tablespoons of white sugar
- salt and pepper to taste.
- One teaspoon of dried oregano

Directions:

1. Set the oven to 350 deg. F. Place the eggplants on a baking sheet, then pierce them with a fork. Bake for at least 1 1/2 hours, or until tender, flipping halfway through. Allow cooling before peeling and dicing.
2. In a large mixing bowl, combine the olive oil, garlic, salt, vinegar, sugar, oregano, parsley, basil, and pepper. Stir in the chopped eggplant to coat. Allow marinating for at least 2 hours before serving.

Per serving: Calories: 95kcal; Fat: 4g; Carbs: 16g; Protein: 3g; Saturated Fat: 1g; Cholesterol: 2mg; Sugar: 4g

100. Mandarin Almond Salad

Difficulty: ★★★☆☆
Preparation time: 20 minutes
Cooking time: 20 minutes
Servings: 8
Ingredients:

- Six thinly sliced green onions,
- 2 (11 ounces) cans of mandarin oranges, drained
- ½ cup of sliced almonds
- 2 tablespoons of white sugar
- ½ cup of olive oil
- One rinsed, dried, chopped head of romaine lettuce -
- ¼ cup of red wine vinegar
- One tablespoon of white sugar
- Ground black pepper; to taste.
- ⅛ Teaspoon of red pepper flakes; crushed.

Directions:

1. Combine the oranges, romaine lettuce, and green onions in a large mixing dish.

In a skillet over medium heat, melt two tablespoons of sugar with the almonds. Cook and whisk until the sugar melts and coats the almonds. Continually stir until the nuts are light brown. Place on a platter and set aside to cool for almost 10 minutes.

2. In a jar with a tight-fitting lid, mix olive oil, red wine vinegar, red pepper flakes, one tablespoon of sugar, and black pepper. Shake well until the sugar is completely dissolved. Toss lettuce with salad dressing just before serving. Sprinkle sugared almonds on top and transfer them to a nice serving dish.

Per serving: Calories: 235kcal; Fat: 17g; Carbs: 20g; Protein: 2g; Saturated Fat: 6g; Cholesterol: 0mg; Sugar: 3g

101. Couscous Salad

Difficulty: ★☆☆☆☆
Preparation time: 10 minutes
Cooking time: 0 minutes
Servings: 8
Ingredients:

- 1/2 teaspoon of ground black pepper
- One red medium bell pepper, 1/4-inch pieces
- 1 cup of zucchini, 1/4-inch pieces
- 1/2 cup of red onion; finely chopped.
- 3/4 teaspoon of ground cumin
- 1 cup of whole-wheat couscous
- 2 tablespoons of olive oil; extra virgin
- Chopped fresh basil, parsley, or oregano for garnish (optional)
- One tablespoon of lemon juice

Directions:

1. Cook the couscous according to the package's directions. When the couscous is done, fluff it up with a fork. Add bell pepper, zucchini, cumin, onion, and black pepper. Put it aside.

2. Whisk together the lemon juice & olive oil in a small bowl. Toss the couscous mixture to mix. Cover and store in the refrigerator. Chill before serving. Fresh herbs may be used as a garnish.

Per serving: Calories: 136kcal; Fat: 4g; Carbs: 21g; Protein: 4g; Saturated Fat: 1g; Cholesterol: 5mg; Sugar: 3g

102. Avocado Watermelon Salad

Difficulty: ★☆☆☆☆
Preparation time: 15 minutes
Cooking time: 0 minutes
Servings: 6 cups
Ingredients:

- Four cups of fresh baby spinach, torn.
- ¼ cup of walnut oil
- 4 cups of cubed watermelon
- ¼ cup of olive oil
- Two large peeled, pitted, diced avocados -
- ½ teaspoon of sweet paprika
- 1 lime, juiced.

Directions:

1. In a mixing bowl, combine the spinach, watermelon, and avocados. Combine walnut oil, lime juice, olive oil, and paprika; pour over the watermelon mixture. Toss to coat evenly.

Per serving: Calories: 350kcal; Fat: 32g; Carbs: 18g; Protein: 3g; Saturated Fat: 8g; Cholesterol: 3mg; Sugar: 2g

103. Tofu Salad

Difficulty: ★☆☆☆☆
Preparation time: 10 minutes
Cooking time: 0 minutes
Servings: 6
Ingredients:
For Salad:

- 1/2-pound lettuce, shredded
- 4 ounces of snow peas
- 1/2 cup carrot, shredded
- 1 cup cabbage, shredded
- 1/2 cup mushrooms, sliced
- 1/2 cup red bell pepper, sliced
- 4 ounces of mung bean sprouts
- 1/2 cup tomato, sliced
- 12 ounces tofu, drained and cubed

For Dressing:

- 1 tablespoon rice vinegar
- 2 tablespoons sesame oil
- Three tablespoons Reduced-Sodium Soy Sauce
- 2 cloves garlic, crushed
- 1 tablespoon sesame seeds
- 1/2 teaspoon ground ginger

Directions:

1. To make the salad: Toss salad ingredients.
2. To make the dressing: Combine dressing ingredients and spoon dressing over salad.

Per serving: Calories: 111kcal; Fat: 6g; Carbs: 54g; Protein: 5g; Saturated Fat: 2g; Cholesterol: 0mg; Sugar: 8g

104. Greek Salad

Difficulty: ★★★☆☆
Preparation time: 20 minutes
Cooking time: 20 minutes
Servings: 8
Ingredients:
For the vinaigrette:

- Two teaspoons of fresh oregano; chopped or 3/4 teaspoon of dried oregano.
- 1 tablespoon of red wine vinegar
- 1/4 teaspoon of black pepper; freshly ground.
- 1 tablespoon of fresh lemon juice

- 2 1/2 tablespoons of olive oil; extra-virgin
- 1/4 teaspoon of salt

For the salad:

- ½ diced red onion,
- One seeded and diced tomato,
- One large, trimmed eggplant, about 1 1/2 pounds, 1/2-inch cubes (about 7 cups)
- Two tablespoons of pitted, black Greek olives; chopped.
- 1-pound stemmed spinach, torn into the bite-sized pieces
- Two tablespoons of feta cheese; crumbled.
- One seeded unpeeled, and diced English (hothouse) cucumber,

Directions:

1. Preheat the oven to 450 deg. F, then place a rack in the bottom third. Use olive oil cooking spray lightly to coat a baking sheet.
2. Mix the lemon juice, vinegar, salt, oregano, and pepper in a small bowl to create the vinaigrette. Slowly drizzle in the olive oil while whisking until emulsified. Set it aside.
3. Arrange the eggplants in one layer on the baking sheet that has been prepared. Using olive oil frying spray, coat the eggplant and roast it for 10 minutes, then for 8 to 10 minutes longer, turn the cubes and roast until softened and gently brown. Allow cooling fully before serving.
4. Combine the cucumber, spinach, onion, tomato, and cooled eggplant in a large mixing basin. Toss the salad gently in the vinaigrette to coat evenly and thoroughly. Distribute the salad among the dishes. Toss in the feta cheese and olives. Serve right away.

Per serving: Calories: 97kcal; Fat: 5g; Carbs: 10g; Protein: 3g; Saturated Fat: 1g; Cholesterol: 2mg; Sugar: 2g

105. Fattoush

Difficulty: ★★☆☆☆
Preparation time: 10 minutes
Cooking time: 10 minutes
Servings: 8
Ingredients:
For the dressing:

- 3 minced garlic cloves,
- 1/4 cup of fresh lemon juice
- 1/2 teaspoon of salt
- 1 teaspoon of ground cumin
- 1/2 teaspoon of red pepper flakes
- One teaspoon of ground sumac (or lemon zest to taste)
- 2 tablespoons of olive oil; extra-virgin
- 1/4 teaspoon of black pepper; freshly ground.

For the salad:

- Three chopped green onions with tender green tops,
- One chopped head of romaine lettuce (about 4 cups)
- One tablespoon of chopped fresh mint.
- 2 (inches in diameter) whole-wheat pitas
- 1 seeded and diced red bell pepper,
- Two seeded and diced tomatoes,
- 1/4 cup of fresh flat-leaf (Italian) parsley; chopped.
- Two seeded, peeled, and diced small cucumbers

Directions:

1. Make the dressing first. In a blender, mix the garlic, lemon juice, cumin, sumac (or lemon zest), red pepper flakes, salt, and black pepper. Blend

until completely smooth. Sprinkle the olive oil in a fine mist while the motor runs until emulsified. Place it aside.

2. After that, make the pita croutons. Preheat the oven to 400 degrees Fahrenheit. Rip each pita into half-inch pieces (or you may cut each into eight triangles). Bring the pieces on a baking sheet in a single layer and bake for 8 minutes, or until crisp and faintly brown. Allow cooling before serving. Now it's time to put the salad together. Toss the tomatoes, lettuce, cucumbers, green onions, mint, bell pepper, and parsley in a large mixing bowl. Toss in the dressing gently to coat evenly. Distribute the salad among the dishes. Add the croutons on top.

Per serving: Calories: 108kcal; Fat: 4g; Carbs: 15g; Protein: 3g; Saturated Fat: 1g; Cholesterol: 0mg; Sugar: 5g

106. Apple-Fennel Slaw

Difficulty: ★★☆☆☆
Preparation time: 15 minutes
Cooking time: 0 minutes
Servings: 4
Ingredients:

- 2 grated carrots,
- One medium-sized thinly sliced fennel bulb
- 2 tablespoons of raisins
- One large thinly sliced and cored Granny Smith apple,
- 4 lettuce leaves
- 1/2 cup of apple juice
- 1 tablespoon of olive oil
- 2 tablespoons of apple cider vinegar
- 1 teaspoon of sugar

Directions:

1. To prepare the slaw, put the carrots, apple, fennel, and raisins in a large mixing bowl. Sprinkle with olive oil,

cover, and chill while preparing the rest of the ingredients.

2. Combine the apple juice and sugar in a small saucepan. Cook, occasionally stirring, until the liquid has been reduced to about 1/4 cup, approximately 10 minutes. Remove from the heat and set aside to cool. Add the apple cider vinegar and mix well. Pour the apple juice mixture over the slaw and toss to blend thoroughly.

3. Allow cooling completely. Serve with lettuce leaves on the side.

Per serving: Calories: 124kcal; Fat: 4g; Carbs: 22g; Protein: 2g; Saturated Fat: 1g; Cholesterol: 0mg; Sugar: 5g

107. Fruited Pistachios Millet Salad

Difficulty: ★★★☆☆
Preparation time: 10 minutes
Cooking time: 15 minutes
Servings: 4
Ingredients:

- 1 cup millet
- ½ cup pistachios, toasted
- ½ cup dried longings
- ½ cup peanuts, toasted
- 2 kiwifruits, diced
- Zest and juice of 2 orange
- 3 tbsps. ruby port
- 2 tbsps. finely chopped turmeric

Directions:

1. Take 2 quarts of lightly salted water to a boil over high heat and pour the millet. Return to a boil, lower the heat to medium, cover, and simmer for 12 to 14 minutes. Drain off the water, rinse the millet until cool, and set aside.

2. Whisk the orange juice, zest, and ruby port in a large bowl. Toss until well combined. Stir in the pistachios, longings, peanuts, kiwifruit, and

turmeric and toss until well combined. Put in the cooked millet and toss to blend. Refrigerate before serving.

Per serving: Calories: 388kcal; Fat: 31g; Carbs: 87g; Protein: 8g; Saturated Fat: 9g; Cholesterol: 0mg; Sugar: 7g

CHAPTER 9: Desserts

108. Lemon Cheesecake

Difficulty: ★★★☆☆
Preparation time: 10 minutes
Cooking time: 20 minutes
Servings: 8
Ingredients:

- One envelope of unflavored gelatin
- 2 tablespoons of cold water
- 1/2 cup of skim milk; heat to boiling point
- 2 tablespoons of lemon juice
- Egg substitute equal to one egg or two egg whites
- 1 teaspoon of vanilla
- 1/4 cup of sugar
- lemon zest
- 2 cups of low-fat cottage cheese

Directions:

1. Combine the gelatin, water, and lemon juice in a blender container. The process takes 1 to 2 minutes at low speed to soften gelatin.
2. Add the boiling milk and process until the gelatin is completely dissolved. Add egg replacement, vanilla, sugar, and cheese to a blender container, and blend until smooth.
3. Fill a 9-inch pie pan or a circular flat dish halfway with the mixture. Refrigerate for 2 to 3 hours. Just before serving, sprinkle with lemon zest if desired.

Per serving: Calories: 80kcal; Fat: 1g; Carbs: 9g; Protein: 9g; Saturated Fat: 0g; Cholesterol: 3mg; Sugar: 6g

109. Apple Dumplings

Difficulty: ★★★☆☆
Preparation time: 2 hours
Cooking time: 30 minutes
Servings: 8
Ingredients:

Dough:

- 2 tablespoons of apple liquor or brandy
- 1 tablespoon of butter
- 2 tablespoons of buckwheat flour
- 1 teaspoon of honey
- Two tablespoons of rolled oats.
- 1 cup of whole-wheat flour

Apple filling:

- 1 teaspoon of nutmeg
- Six large thinly sliced tart apples,
- Zest of 1 lemon
- 2 tablespoons of honey

Directions:

1. Preheat the oven to 350 degrees Fahrenheit. Combine the flour, honey, butter, and oats in a food processor. Pulse a few times more 'til the mixture resembles a fine meal.
2. Pulse a few more times to incorporate the brandy or apple liquor until the mixture begins to form a ball. Refrigerate it for two hours after removing the mixture from the food processor. Combine nutmeg, apples, and honey. Toss in the lemon zest. Set it aside.
3. Extra flour is used to roll out the chilled dough to a thickness of 1/4 inch. Using an 8-inch circle cutter, cut the dough into 8-inch circles.
4. Use an 8-cup muffin pan that has been gently sprayed with cooking spray. Place a dough circle over each gently sprayed

cup. Gently press dough into place. Fill them with the apple mixture. To seal, fold over the edges, squeeze the top, and bake for 30 minutes or golden brown.

Per serving: Calories: 178kcal; Fat: 3g; Carbs: 36g; Protein: 3g; Saturated Fat: 1g; Cholesterol: 4mg; Sugar: 5g

110. Whole-Grain Mixed Berry Coffeecake

Difficulty: ★★★☆☆
Preparation time: 10 minutes
Cooking time: 30 minutes
Servings: 8
Ingredients:

- 1 tablespoon of vinegar
- 1/2 cup of skim milk
- 1 teaspoon of vanilla
- 2 tablespoons of canola oil
- 1/3 cup of packed brown sugar
- 1 egg
- 1/2 teaspoon of ground cinnamon
- 1 cup of pastry flour; whole-wheat
- 1/2 teaspoon of baking soda
- 1/8 teaspoon of salt
- 1/4 cup of low-fat slightly crushed granola,
- 1 cup of frozen mixed berries, such as raspberries, blueberries, and blackberries

Directions:

1. Preheat the oven to 350 degrees Fahrenheit. Use a cooking spray to coat a cake pan or 8-inch round and coat it with flour.
2. Combine the vinegar, milk, oil, egg, vanilla, and brown sugar in a large mixing bowl and whisk until smooth. Stir in flour, cinnamon, baking soda, and salt until moistened. Fold half of the berries into the batter gently. Pour into the pan that has been prepared. Lastly,

top with the granola and remaining berries.

3. Bake for 25 to 30 minutes, or until golden brown and the center of the top snaps back when touched. Cool for 10 minutes in the pan on a cooling rack. Warm the dish before serving.

Per serving: Calories: 165kcal; Fat: 5g; Carbs: 26g; Protein: 4g; Saturated Fat: 1g; Cholesterol: 24mg; Sugar: 8g

111. Rustic Apple-Cranberry Tart

Difficulty: ★★★☆☆
Preparation time: 10 minutes
Cooking time: 50 minutes
Servings: 8
Ingredients:
For the filling:

- 1/4 cup of apple juice
- 1/2 cup of dried cranberries
- 1/4 teaspoon of ground cinnamon
- 2 tablespoons of corn starch
- 1 teaspoon of vanilla extract
- Four large cored, peeled, sliced tart apples,

For the crust:

- 2 teaspoons of sugar
- 1 1/4 cups of whole-wheat flour (wholemeal)
- 1/4 cup of ice water
- Three tablespoons of trans-free margarine

Directions:

1. Combine the apple juice and cranberries in a small microwave-safe bowl. Cook for 1 minute on high, then stir. Cover and leave aside for 1 hour until the mixture is near room temperature. Continue to cook the apple juice for 30 seconds, tossing after each interval, until it is extremely warm.

2. Preheat the oven to 375 degrees Fahrenheit. Combine the apple slices and cornstarch in a large mixing bowl. Toss well to get an equal coating. Add juice and cranberries to a mixing bowl. Mix thoroughly. Add cinnamon and vanilla to a mixing bowl. Put it aside.

3. In a large mixing bowl, combine flour and sugar to make the crust. Add sliced margarine into the mixture and mix well until crumbly. Add one tablespoon of ice water and stir with a fork until the dough forms a rough lump.

4. Bring a big sheet of aluminum foil to the surface and tape it down. It should be dusted with flour. Flatten the dough in the middle of the foil. Roll the dough from the center to the edges with a rolling pin to form a 13-inch-diameter circle. Add fruit filling in the dough's middle. Cover the dough with the filling, leaving about a 1-2 inch border. Fold the crust's top and bottom edges up over the filling. The pastry will not completely cover the contents; it should have a rustic appearance.

5. Remove the foil and the countertop from the tape. Cover the tart with another piece of foil to cover the exposed fruit. Slide the tart onto a baking sheet, top and bottom foil, and bake for 30 minutes. Remove the foil from the top and bake for another 10 minutes or browned. Serve immediately after cutting into eight wedges.

Per serving: Calories: 197kcal; Fat: 5g; Carbs: 35g; Protein: 3g; Saturated Fat: 2g; Cholesterol: 0mg; Sugar: 11g

112. Mango Popsicles

Difficulty: ★★☆☆☆
Preparation time: 10 minutes
Cooking time: 5 minutes
Servings: 6
Ingredients:

- 2 mangoes, peeled & diced
- 2 tbsp maple syrup
- 1 lime juice
- 14 oz can coconut milk

Directions:

1. Add mangoes, maple syrup, lime juice, and coconut milk into the blender and blend until smooth.

2. Pour mango mixture into the popsicle molds and place in the refrigerator until set.

3. Serve chilled and enjoy.

Per serving: Calories: 221kcal; Fat: 15g; Carbs: 25g; Protein: 2g; Saturated Fat: 5g; Cholesterol: 0mg; Sugar: 21g

113. Carrot And Spice Quick Bread

Difficulty: ★★★★☆
Preparation time: 15 minutes
Cooking time: 45 minutes
Servings: 17
Ingredients:

- 1 cup of whole-wheat flour
- One teaspoon of grated orange rind
- 1/2 cup of all-purpose flour; sifted.
- One tablespoon of walnuts, finely chopped.
- 1/4 cup and two tablespoons of brown sugar; firmly packed
- 1/2 teaspoon of ground cinnamon
- 1 1/2 cups of shredded carrots
- 1/4 teaspoon of ground ginger
- ½ tablespoon of golden raisins
- 1/2 teaspoon of baking soda
- 1/3 cup of skim milk
- One beaten egg whites/ egg substitute equal to 1 egg,
- 1 teaspoon of vanilla extract
- ¾ tablespoons of unsweetened orange juice

- 1/3 cup of margarine; trans-fat-free, softened.
- ½ teaspoon of baking powder

Directions:

1. Preheat the oven to 375 degrees Fahrenheit. Cooking spray coats a 2 ½ by 4 ½ by 8 ½ inch loaf pan.
2. Combine the dry flours, baking soda, powder, cinnamon, and ginger in a small dish and set them aside.
3. Mix margarine and sugar in a large bowl using an electric mixer or hand. Add orange juice, milk, vanilla, egg, and orange rind to a mixing bowl. Stir in raisins, carrots, and walnuts in a mixing bowl. Add dry ingredients that have been set aside. Mix thoroughly.
4. Preheat the oven to 350°F and bake for about 45 mins, or until a wooden pick inserted in the middle comes out clean. Pour the batter into the loaf pan. Allow 10 minutes to cool in the pan. Remove the pan from the oven, then cool fully on a wire rack.

Per serving: Calories: 110kcal; Fat: 5g; Carbs: 15g; Protein: 2g; Saturated Fat: 1g; Cholesterol: 3mg; Sugar: 7g

114. Grapes And Lemon Sour Cream Sauce

Difficulty: ★★☆☆☆
Preparation time: 10 minutes
Cooking time: 0 minutes
Servings: 6
Ingredients:

- 2 tablespoons of powdered sugar
- 1/2 cup of sour cream; fat-free
- 1/2 teaspoon of lemon zest
- 1/8 teaspoon of vanilla extract
- 1/2 teaspoon of lemon juice
- 1 1/2 cups of seedless red grapes
- Three tablespoons of chopped walnuts
- 1 1/2 cups of seedless green grapes

Directions:

1. Combine lemon juice, powdered sugar, sour cream, lemon zest, and vanilla in a small mixing bowl. To ensure an equal distribution of ingredients, whisk them together. Refrigerate for several hours after covering.
2. In six stemmed dessert cups or bowls, place equal parts of grapes, and top each dish with a dollop of sauce and 1/2 spoonful of chopped walnuts. Serve right away.

Per serving: Calories: 106kcal; Fat: 2g; Carbs: 20g; Protein: 2g; Saturated Fat: 0g; Cholesterol: 2mg; Sugar: 9g

115. Strawberries And Cream

Difficulty: ★★☆☆☆
Preparation time: 10 minutes
Cooking time: 0 minutes
Servings: 6
Ingredients:

- 1/2 cup of brown sugar
- 1 1/2 cups of sour cream; fat-free
- 1 quart fresh hulled and halved strawberries; (6 whole for garnish)
- 2 tablespoons of amaretto liqueur

Directions:

1. Whisk the brown sugar, sour cream, and liqueur in a small bowl.
2. Combine the sour cream mixture and halved strawberries in a large mixing bowl. To combine, carefully stir everything together. Cover, then chill for 1 hour or until well cooked.
3. Fill six chilled sherbet glasses or colored bowls halfway with strawberries. Serve immediately with whole strawberries as a garnish.

Per serving: Calories: 136kcal; Fat: 3g; Carbs: 31g; Protein: 3g; Saturated Fat: 1g; Cholesterol: 6mg; Sugar: 6g

116. Healthy Summer Yogurt

Difficulty: ★★☆☆☆
Preparation time: 10 minutes
Cooking time: 5 minutes
Servings: 6
Ingredients:

- 2 cups frozen berries
- 1 tsp vanilla
- ½ cup Greek yogurt
- 2 tbsp maple syrup
- 2 frozen bananas

Directions:

1. Bring all ingredients into the blender and blend until smooth.
2. Pour blended mixture into the air-tight container, cover, and place in the freezer for 3 hours.
3. Serve chilled and enjoy.

Per serving: Calories: 99kcal; Fat: 2g; Carbs: 19g; Protein: 3g; Saturated Fat: 0g; Cholesterol: 4mg; Sugar: 15g

117. Chocolate Yogurt

Difficulty: ★★☆☆☆
Preparation time: 5 minutes
Cooking time: 5 minutes
Servings: 1
Ingredients:

- 1 cup Greek yogurt
- 1 tbsp unsweetened soy milk
- 1 tsp maple syrup
- 2 tbsp unsweetened cocoa powder

Directions:

1. Bring all ingredients into the blender, then blend until smooth.
2. Pour blended mixture into the air-tight container, cover, and place in the freezer for 3 hours.
3. Serve chilled and enjoy.

Per serving: Calories: 200kcal; Fat: 6g; Carbs: 20g; Protein: 22g; Saturated Fat: 2g; Cholesterol: 10mg; Sugar: 14g

118. Delicious & Healthy Rice Pudding

Difficulty: ★★☆☆☆
Preparation time: 10 minutes
Cooking time: 15 minutes
Servings: 4
Ingredients:

- 4 cups cooked black rice
- 1 tbsp vanilla
- 3 dates, pitted & chopped
- ½ cup frozen blueberries
- ½ cup frozen raspberries
- 1 cup frozen strawberries
- ¾ cup dried cherries, diced
- 4 cups unsweetened coconut milk

Directions:

1. Add cooked rice and remaining ingredients into the saucepan and bring to a boil.
2. Turn the heat to low and simmer for 15 minutes.
3. Stir well and serve.

Per serving: Calories: 84kcal; Fat: 58g; Carbs: 75g; Protein: 13g; Saturated Fat: 9g; Cholesterol: 2mg; Sugar: 24g

119. Baked Figs

Difficulty: ★★☆☆☆
Preparation time: 5 minutes
Cooking time: 15 minutes
Servings: 8
Ingredients:

- 8 figs, quarters
- ¼ cup maple syrup

Directions:

1. Preheat the oven to 350 deg. F.
2. Arrange figs onto a parchment-lined baking sheet, drizzle with maple syrup,

and bake in a preheated oven for 10-15 minutes.

3. Serve and enjoy.

Per serving: Calories: 80kcal; Fat: 1g; Carbs: 21g; Protein: 1g; Saturated Fat: 0g; Cholesterol: 0mg; Sugar: 18g

120. Healthy Quinoa Pudding

Difficulty: ★★☆☆☆
Preparation time: 10 minutes
Cooking time: 18 minutes
Servings: 2
Ingredients:

- 2/3 cup quinoa, rinsed
- ¼ tsp cinnamon
- 2 tbsp agave syrup
- 1 tsp vanilla
- 1 cup unsweetened soy milk
- Pinch of salt

Directions:

1. Add quinoa, milk, and remaining ingredients into the saucepan and cook over medium heat until pudding is thickened and quinoa is cooked.
2. Stir well and serve.

Per serving: Calories: 288kcal; Fat: 5g; Carbs: 51g; Protein: 8g; Saturated Fat: 1g; Cholesterol: 0mg; Sugar: 12g

CHAPTER 10: 30-Day Low-Cholesterol Meal Plan

Days	Breakfast	Lunch	Dinner	Dessert
1	Tofu And Cucumber Spring Rolls	Honey Soy Tilapia	Grilled Chicken Salad With Olives And Oranges	Mango Popsicles
2	Protein Cereal	Chicken, Mushroom, And Bell Pepper Skewers	Butternut Squash And Apple Salad	Strawberries And Cream
3	Vegetarian Scramble	Ambrosia With Coconut And Toasted Almonds	Fish Tacos	Grapes And Lemon Sour Cream Sauce
4	Nutritious Roasted Chickpeas	Loaded Veggie-Stuffed Peppers	Lemon Chicken And Asparagus	Apple Dumplings
5	Cranberry Hotcakes	Farfalle With Asparagus And Smoked Salmon	Broccoli Wild Rice Casserole	Whole-Grain Mixed Berry Coffeecake
6	Italian Baked Omelet	Italian Chicken Bake	Mediterranean Patties	Delicious & Healthy Rice Pudding
7	Rolled Oats Cereal	Spinach, Walnut, And Black Bean Burgers	Grilled Vegetable Orzo Salad	Healthy Quinoa Pudding
8	Egg Foo Young	Juicy Burgers	Maple-Garlic Salmon And Cauliflower Sheet Pan Dinner	Carrot And Spice Quick Bread
9	Vegetable Omelet	Spicy Honey Chicken And Eggplant	Cashew Chicken	Healthy Summer Yogurt
10	Nuts And Seeds Trail Mix	Chicken Rice	Balsamic Blueberry Chicken	Baked Figs
11	Nutty Oat Cereal	Cod With Italian Crumb Topping	Chicken Curry	Rustic Apple-Cranberry Tart
12	Maghrebi Poached Eggs	One Pan Chicken	Steak And Vegetables With Chimichurri Sauce	Lemon Cheesecake
13	Lean Beef Lettuce Wraps	Mexican Stuffed Peppers With Corn And Black Beans	Tailgate Chili	Chocolate Yogurt
14	Breakfast Splits	Meatloaf	Grilled Scallops With Gremolata	Old Bay Crispy Kale Chips

15	Creamed Rice	Mexican Skillet Meal	Mango Black Bean Salsa	Winter Perfect Guacamole
16	Avo Bruschetta	Artichokes Alla Romana	Flank Steak With Caramelized Onions	Strawberries And Cream
17	Italian Baked Omelet	Citrus Swordfish With Citrus Salsa	Lentils And Pasta	Grapes And Lemon Sour Cream Sauce
18	Rolled Oats Cereal	Italian Chicken Bake	Bbq Pulled Pork With Greek Yogurt Slaw	Nutty Broccoli Slaw
19	Egg Foo Young	Oaxacan Tacos	Fish Tacos	Honey-Lime Berry Salad
20	Vegetable Omelet	Steak And Vegetables With Chimichurri Sauce	Spicy Trout Sheet Pan Dinner	Delicious & Healthy Rice Pudding
21	Tofu And Cucumber Spring Rolls	Lime Turkey Skewers	Chicken, Mushroom, And Bell Pepper Skewers	Healthy Quinoa Pudding
22	Protein Cereal	Chicken Curry	Piña Colada Chicken	Curried Cannellini Bean Dip
23	Vegetarian Scramble	Sweet Salad Dressing Chicken And Carrot Sheet Pan Dinner	Honey Soy Tilapia	Healthy Beet Dip
24	Nuts And Seeds Trail Mix	Farfalle With Asparagus And Smoked Salmon	Iron Packed Turkey	Baked Figs
25	Nutty Oat Cereal	Red Wine Chicken	Cashew Chicken	Rustic Apple-Cranberry Tart
26	Maghrebi Poached Eggs	Steak And Vegetables With Chimichurri Sauce	Salmon Salad	Cannellini Bean Hummus
27	Lean Beef Lettuce Wraps	Turkey Oat Patties	Lime Chicken Wraps	Crispy Carrot Fries
28	Cranberry Hotcakes	Yellow Pear And Cherry Tomato Salad	Chipotle Lime Avocado Salad	Carrot And Spice Quick Bread
29	Italian Baked Omelet	Salmon Patties	Ambrosia With Coconut And Toasted Almonds	Healthy Summer Yogurt
30	Breakfast Splits	Mexican Skillet Meal	English Cucumber Salad With Balsamic Vinaigrette	Pita Chips

Conclusion

The risk of cardiovascular disease increases in proportion to the total cholesterol level. These conditions include coronary artery disease, a form of heart disease. It is also due to the elevation in LDL cholesterol levels and lower HDL cholesterol levels, often accompanied by increased blood sugar levels.

Many people have tried to deter their bad cholesterol with diet and exercise, but it is still very high in many cases. Many people believe that there is no benefit from eating plant-based foods when weight loss occurs because the body automatically burns mostly fat for fuel instead of sugar. However, this depends on how efficiently and effectively a person can utilize dietary choices to lower bad cholesterol and maintain a healthy weight.

"A scientific study revealed that the optimum diet for lowering cholesterol is a plant-based diet, which is very low in saturated fat and cholesterol. The study group was made of men and women with normal LDL cholesterol levels, averaging 120 milligrams per deciliter (mg/dL) with an average weight of 200 pounds. Over six weeks, the subjects were asked to limit animal products and increase plant-based foods to about 50% or more of total calories."

The results showed that LDL levels fell from an average of 130 to 107 over the course of 6 weeks. The HDL levels remained constant at an average of 60 mg/dL. However, the LDL levels fell in all participants regardless of age or weight. This excludes that people may have different levels of good cholesterol, which are not measured, or what is measured as HDL may be bad cholesterol.

The study confirmed that a low-fat diet was beneficial for lowering bad cholesterol. It also showed the ability to reduce LDL and maintain good HDL levels with a plant-based diet. The study group performed extremely well and will probably attribute this outcome to their healthy lifestyle choices.

It is still important to note that drugs have much higher success rates when prescribed than when used as self-prescribed supplements, like statin medication. Many people have tried to lower bad cholesterol with diet and exercise, but it is still very high in many cases. Many people believe that there is no benefit from eating plant-based foods when weight loss occurs because the body automatically burns mostly fat for fuel instead of sugar. However, this depends on how efficiently and effectively a person can utilize dietary choices to lower bad cholesterol and maintain a healthy weight.

Index

Mexican Stuffed Peppers with Corn and Black Beans; 43
Nutritious Roasted Chickpeas; 26
Nuts And Seeds Trail Mix; 23
Nutty Broccoli Slaw; 56
Nutty Oat Cereal; 21
Oaxacan Tacos; 44
Old Bay Crispy Kale Chips; 56
One Pan Chicken; 38
Piña Colada Chicken; 32
Pita Chips; 57
Potato Salad; 64
Potato Squash Soup; 53
Protein Cereal; 20
Red Wine Chicken; 35
Rolled Oats Cereal; 24
Rustic Apple-Cranberry Tart; 71
Salmon Patties; 30
Salmon Salad; 27
Silky Zucchini Soup; 55

Spicy Almonds; 58
Spicy Honey Chicken and Eggplant; 33
Spicy Trout Sheet Pan Dinner; 29
Spinach Berry Salad; 63
Spinach, Walnut, and Black Bean Burgers; 46
Steak and Vegetables with Chimichurri Sauce; 41
Strawberries And Cream; 73
Sweet Salad Dressing Chicken and Carrot Sheet Pan Dinner; 32
Tailgate Chili; 45
Tofu and Cucumber Spring Rolls; 22
Tofu Salad; 66
Turkey Oat Patties; 39
Vegetable Omelet; 21
Vegetarian Scramble; 23
Waldorf Salad with Yogurt; 62
Whole-Grain Mixed Berry Coffeecake; 71
Winter Perfect Guacamole; 60
Yellow Pear and Cherry Tomato Salad; 49